SCIENTIFI(

CW00403083

The European Union, Turkey and Islam

Amsterdam University Press, Amsterdam 2004

Illustration front cover: Reza/Webistan/Corbis/TCS

ISBN 90-5356-712-7

CONTENTS

The European Union, Turkey and Islam

3

4

SUMMARY

Officially, Islam does not play a role in the decision whether to accept
Turkey as a member state of the European Union (EU). Yet many people
wonder if a Muslim country such as Turkey would really fit into the European Union. Is Turkish Islam compatible with democracy, human rights
and the separation of state and religion? The central question of this report,
therefore, is whether the fact that the majority of its population is Muslim
forms a hindrance to Turkish accession to the European Union.

This report is a full translation of *De Europese Unie, Turkije en de islam*,
that was officially presented to the Dutch government on 21 June 2004 by
the Netherlands Scientific Council for Government Policy. The Council
is an independent advisory body for the Dutch government which
provides sollicited and unsollicited advise on developments which may
affect society in the long term (see also: www.wrr.nl).

Reason
The question examined in this report is highly relevant, given the decision
to be taken by the EU under the Dutch Presidency in December 2004.
It will then be decided whether candidate member state Turkey has made
sufficient progress towards meeting the so-called political Copenhagen
criterion that accession negotiations can commence. This criterion stipu-
lates a stable democracy and a constitutional state that guarantees the rule
of law, human rights and the rights of minorities.

Religion as such plays no role in this Copenhagen criterion. The fact that
the majority of the Turkish population is Muslim, therefore, played no formal role in the decision taken in 1999 to grant Turkey the status of candidate
member. However, especially since the terrorist attacks on 11 September
2001, the concerns in member states about Islam and Muslims have increased. This has contributed to growing doubts over the question whether
Turkey's Islamic character is compatible with the political achievements of
the EU and its member states. Objections to membership, on cultural and
religious ground, have been increasingly raised, even in political circles.

Objective of the report
In light of these recent discussions, the Netherlands Scientific Council
for Government Policy (henceforth identified by the initials of its Dutch
title – the WRR) considers it important to have a separate review of the
question whether Turkish Islam is compatible with the values upon which
the Union is based. In this way, the WRR hopes to contribute to the formu-
lation of an informed judgement .

In this report, the WRR offers the government no advice on the question whether accession negotiations should now be started with Turkey. The decision that will have to be made in December will have to take full account of all aspects of the membership question. This report makes no such comprehensive assessment; it is confined exclusively to the relationship between Turkish Islam and the democratic constitutional state.

Nonetheless, the WRR, at the end of this report, looks at the possible implications of Turkish membership for the deteriorating relations between the Muslim world and the West.

Religion in the European Union and its member states

In answering the question whether Turkish Islam forms a hindrance to EU membership, we should first determine the position of religion in the EU itself. Religion does not form part of the common EU values. The Union has defined itself as a system of values and actions based on the basic principles of freedom and democracy, as well as a recognition of human rights, fundamental liberties and the rule of law. The *freedom* of thought, conscience and religion forms an integral part of these basic rights, as does the respect afforded by the Union to cultural and religious diversity.

Viewed from the perspective of the principles and fundamental rights of the Union, there is no a priori reason to exclude a country on the grounds of its dominant religion. However, the question of the separation of church and state is another matter altogether. Behind the principles and the political and civil rights of the Union lies the assumption that its member states have a constitutional state that recognises and guarantees both the autonomy of church and state, and freedom of religion and conscience. The principle of autonomy implies that religious communities and the state each have separate areas of competence. Freedom of religion and conscience means that religious believers (including members of minority churches), atheists and apostates face no restrictions in the exercise of their rights. It is precisely in this area that people harbour doubts about Islam.

Looking at the autonomy of church and state, the situation among EU member states is extremely diverse. Even though all member states are formally secular and recognise freedom of religion, they do not always remain neutral towards religions or religious denominations. For example, some states have a state church and others do not. Even where there is no state church, one denomination may in practice be privileged above others. On the other hand, recognising a state church does not necessarily exclude equal treatment of other churches. Each member state has its own, often tense, history in the relationship between church, state, politics and society, which has resulted in specific arrangements. Thus, on the question of the separation of church and state there is no single European model against which to test the Turkish experience. The most that can be done is to see whether Turkey meets certain minimum conditions.

Characteristics of Turkish Islam

The next question is whether Turkish Islam has characteristics that stand in the way of the country's accession. In other words, are there developments afoot in Turkey that would negatively influence the attitude of Turkish Islam towards essential EU values? The WRR's answer to this question is negative. The Turkish state is constitutionally protected against religious influences. In this respect the country has the same rigorous separation between the state and religion as does France. Indeed, France's so-called *laicism* provided the model for the constitution of the Republic of Turkey. However, unlike the French state, the Turkish state still exercises a strong control and influence over religion.

These characteristics have a long history. The nineteenth century was a period of modernisation following the West European example. The French Enlightenment greatly influenced constitutional thinking also in the Ottoman period. Not long after West European states had done so, Turkey established its first constitution and held elections for the first Ottoman parliament (1876). This was followed, until the First World War, by a period of highly religiously coloured nationalism, which was accompanied by much government interference in the contents and the propagation of religious beliefs. The Turkish Republic was established in 1923, and it marked the beginning of the most extreme banning of religious influences on the state. The Kemalist movement, named after the founder of the Republic, Mustafa Kemal Pasja (Atatürk), rigorously consigned religion to the private sphere. It banned religious symbols from public life, abolished religious organisations or placed them under state control, and outlawed the popular mystical orders. This period also witnessed the replacement of the last remnants of Islamic law, namely family law, by secular law. Islamic criminal law had already been abolished in the middle of the nineteenth century. After the Second World War, Turkey introduced a multi-party democracy and Islam gradually became a major political factor, even in programmes of non-religious secular parties. In addition, from the 1960s onwards, political parties also emerged that explicitly identified themselves as Islamic.

The WRR considers that the rise of Islam as a *politically* relevant phenomenon should be seen in the context of its forced marginalisation in the previous decades. This denial of Islamic identity by the upper classes was never shared by the population at large. At the same time, this rise was underpinned by important socio-economic changes in Turkey, such as the development of a substantial middle class in rural areas and in the smaller

7

towns, for whom Islam constitutes a normal part of everyday life. Until now, Islamic parties have been met by profound distrust from the establishment in and around governmental institutions, who identify strongly with Kemalist thinking. Both the Constitutional Court and the armed forces have intervened on several occasions and banned such parties. Since 1982, as a counterweight to the radical left and religious views, the army institutionalised a form of 'state-Islam' which still enjoys a privileged position today. This version of state religion combines a strong emphasis on social conservatism and nationalism with a moderate version of Islam and is propagated through mosques and through compulsory religious education in schools. This state-Islam, which is firmly embedded in a secular state system and which reflects the beliefs of the majority of the population and of conservative political bodies, has given recognition to the importance attached to Islam by the broad public.

Finally, the WRR notes that for the new Islamic political parties that were created during the last decade, the principle of the separation of state and religion was an important conditioning factor. However, they attached different consequences to it. Although they accepted the secular state, they also wanted to increase the freedom of religion and therefore opposed the strong government controls on religion. Whilst supporting the existing democratic system, they have fought to make it accessible to religion-based parties. They still consider freedom of conscience and freedom of expression as the basis of democracy and human rights. They have contested neither the secular nature of the law, nor the principle of equal rights for men and women.

While it is possible to view this emphasis on such freedoms as a mere effort to enlarge the legitimate scope for one's own views, the current government party, the Justice and Development Party (AK Party), which itself grew from a government banned Islamic party, emphasises human rights even more strongly from the standpoint of pluralism. The party intrinsically values differences in religion, culture, and opinions and sees secularism as the principle of freedom that makes their exercise and expression possible.

Conclusion of the WRR

The WRR believes that the fact that Turkey is a country with a majority Muslim population is no hindrance to its EU accession. This conclusion is based on the following considerations.

First, the WRR has established, on the basis of the developments described above and the current characteristics of Turkish Islam, that the principle of the secular democratic state is solidly rooted in Turkish society. Moreover, the development of the secular state in Turkey shows many parallels with West European history and it was also more or less concomitant. The existence of Islam in Turkey did not stand in the way of these developments but instead, right to the present day, helped to encourage them. The fact that the democratisation process after the Second World War should have been accompanied by the emergence of Islam as an important political force, is a normal phenomenon. When we see the political role still played by religion in many European states, it is not surprising that the Kemalist movement failed to ban religion entirely from the political and public sphere.

However, from an EU perspective the issue of Islam in Turkey is not so much a problem of the influence of religion on the state as a problem of the influence of the state on religion. This is because government intervention in religion is stronger in Turkey than in EU member states, even though some EU countries also recognise a state religion. Moreover, the constitutional restrictions on the democratic process aimed at protecting the secular state system, are incompatible with the principles of the EU. This observation applies equally to the role of the military as a guardian of this system. It is here that the European Parliament and the European Commission would like to see important changes implemented.

9

Nonetheless, the WRR considers that there is no indication that Turkish Islam will lose its moderate character, and thus endanger the secular democratic state, if state restrictions are relaxed or if the military gradually withdraw from politics, as advocated by the current Turkish government. The great majority of the population wants nothing to do with fundamentalism and religious intolerance and expresses a preference for moderate political parties. They support the secular character of the state and reject any introduction of Islamic law. For these reasons, violent Islamic fundamentalism has few followers in Turkey.

Structure of this report

The first section contains the report of the WRR to the Dutch government. Chapter 1 presents the reason for and the key question of the report. Chapter 2 examines the position of religion in the EU and arrangements that exist within member states governing the relationship between the state, religion, politics and society. Chapter 3 describes developments in Turkey that explain the Turkish position towards the EU's essential values. In chapter 4, the WRR presents its conclusions. This is followed by an epilogue on the possible implications of Turkish membership for the difficult relationship between the Muslim world and the West. Part 2 of the report contains the survey 'Searching for the Fault-Line', commissioned by the WRR, in which prof. dr. E.J. Zürcher and H. van der Linden present their analysis on Turkish Islam and the EU.

PREFACE

This report has been prepared by an internal project group of the Netherlands Scientific Council for Government Policy (WRR) comprising researchers dr. W. Asbeek Brusse and drs. I.J. Schoonenboom.

The analyses in the report are based, in part, on a study conducted by prof. dr. E.J. Zürcher and H. van der Linden at the request of the Netherlands Scientific Council for Government Policy. The study, *Searching for the Fault-Line. A Survey of the role of Turkish Islam in Turkey's accession to the EU in the light of the 'clash of civilisations'*, is also published in this volume.

The WRR assumes full responsibility for its "Report to the Government". The authors of the commissioned study are entirely responsible for their own views.

1   INTRODUCTION

1.1   BACKGROUND AND MOTIVATION

The debate on Turkey

During the Dutch Presidency of the European Union (EU) in the final six
months of 2004, the EU will have to decide on whether to open membership negotiations with candidate member state Turkey. Officially, that
decision depends on whether the country enjoys a stable constitutional
democracy that guarantees the rule of law, human rights and minority
rights – the so-called political Copenhagen criterion.[1] In the public debate,
however, other considerations have also played a role. Besides the many
practical objections to Turkish membership (the country's size, poverty,
rural nature or its many unstable neighbours), objections of a cultural-religious nature are increasingly being raised. In short, Turkey is alleged to
have a different cultural-religious history from that of 'Europe' and an
incompatible value system.[2]

Up to now, the national governments of the member states, the European Commission and the European Parliament have nearly all adopted
a wait-and-see attitude towards this debate. Insofar as issues of
culture and religion play a role for politicians and 'EU-watchers', it
involves the question whether Turkey is able to guarantee religious
liberties.[3] Hardly any of them have questioned outright whether an
Islamic country such as Turkey fits in with the EU's 'Judeo-Christian
value system'. This reticence is perhaps understandable. After Turkey
became an associate EU partner in 1963, European heads of government
elevated its status to an 'EU candidate country' at the end of 1999
(see also text box 1.1). In doing so, they have already committed themselves in principle to a possible Turkish membership. Moreover, one
would expect representatives of secular states especially to maintain
some distance from making substantive judgements on religious issues
(see sect. 2.3).

Even so, Turkey's Islamic character will inevitably become entwined in
the political decision-making process. The German Christian-Democrats,
for example, have already stated that they will make the question of Turkish accession a core issue in debates on the EU's future. Should accession
negotiations with Turkey indeed begin and be successfully concluded,
the issue will again become politically relevant in the not too distant
future. This is because the accession treaty with the Union will have to
be ratified by all member states either through referenda, or by the
approval of national parliaments. The perception of Turkish Islam and

15

Muslims among parliamentarians and the electorate will, therefore, inevitably play a role in the accession debates.

Turkey, Islam and Muslims

The poor integration of some groups of Muslims in the EU member states, the growing assertiveness of second-generation Muslims, and the world-wide rise of fundamentalism and Islamic terrorism, have placed 'Islam' and 'Muslims' in an increasingly controversial position. In 1999, when the European Council, in the wake of the historic decision on the EU's eastward expansion, also decided to grant Turkey candidate-membership status, '9-11' had yet to happen. The attacks dramatically changed the social and political climate and awoke dormant feelings of deep unease. Subsequently, much of the discourse on relations between Western and Muslim states was cast in the mould of the 'clash of civilisations', to use the phrase coined by Samuel Huntington (Huntington 1993 and 1996). Ethnic violence became more quickly associated with Islam and visible communities of religious Muslims more quickly labelled as dangerous fundamentalists. The March 2004 attacks in Madrid have strengthened this tendency.

It is too easy to trivialise this fear of Islam. It is not only in the Netherlands and the other member states, but also in Turkey itself, that public and political manifestations of Islam raise controversy. Evidence for this can be found in the countless 'headscarf incidents' in Turkey, as well as in the periodic interventions by the Turkish army against democratically elected leaders with overt religious affiliations. Many supporters of Turkish nationalist and secular parties fear that it is precisely the religious fundamentalists who would be given free rein should the military, as a result of EU pressure, be forced to withdraw completely from politics. They are wary of demands by the European Parliament that Turkey should adopt a 'more relaxed position' towards Islam in particular and religion in general. Other groups, too, such as emancipated young women, atheists and gays, distrust the current government of the moderately religious AK Party, and expect that, at any moment, it will show its 'true anti-secularist' colours.

Examples from Dutch, European and Turkish contexts reveal a huge gulf between the broad public debate on 'Islam' and Muslim fundamentalism, on the one hand, and the discussion among European experts and academics on the authoritarian-secular character of the Turkish state, on the other. The former usually gets mired in platitudes about Islam, Muslims, violence and fundamentalism, that do scant justice to the characteristics of Turkish Islam, culture and society. The second debate brings together two different perspectives: one stressing the partiality of the guarantees that Turkey offers for the protection of individuals and (religious) minority groups; the other emphasising the opportunity afforded for the

EU, via Turkish membership, to build a bridge to the Islamic world. Both debates form parts of a wider and more complex issue, namely Turkey's search for a new balance between religion, state and society in a rapidly changing environment. How this search develops, and more particularly which opportunities and threats Turkey will meet en route, are directly relevant to the question whether Islamic Turkey is compatible with membership of the EU. Indirectly, the question is also relevant for Europe's relationship with the Islamic world.

1.2   AIMS, CORE QUESTION AND LIMITATIONS

Aims and core question

This report intends to contribute to an informed discussion on Turkish Islam. In light of the recent discussions, the WRR considers it important to pose this question separately. The core question is:

Does the fact that the majority of Turkey's population is Muslim, form an impediment to Turkey's accession to the European Union?

The following subquestions provide a guideline for answering this core question:

1 How do the EU and its member states deal with religion?
2 What (implicit) requirements does the EU have towards the position of religion in the member states?
3 What do these requirements imply for Turkish Islam and its role in Turkey?
4 To what conclusion do answers to these questions lead on the issue of Turkey's accession to the EU?

The core question of the report could easily give rise to the impression that we are in favour of an additional test for Turkish membership by adding a new, 'religious', component to the political Copenhagen criterion. This is emphatically not the case. Rather, we are concerned to make explicit the underlying assumptions on religion implied in the political Copenhagen criterion. The *formal* requirement for a democratic constitutional state assumes, in the current European context, that church and state are autonomous (this is also referred to as secularism), and that the state guarantees religious freedoms and rights.[4] In this light, the position of religion in relation to state and society in Turkey is relevant as *one component of* the existing political Copenhagen criterion, but certainly not *as a supplement* to it. By studying Turkish Islam separately and explicitly, in the light of the legitimate requirements of a secular, democratic constitutional state, we hope to forestall a situation whereby the decision on Turkish membership would be overshadowed by vague feelings of unease, implicit arguments or unstated, religiously-coloured expectations which the country could never reasonably be expected to fulfil. Unlike the European Commission, we pay extensive attention to the development of the relationship between Turkish Islam and the secular state, as well as to its historical foundations. Further, we examine the rapidly changing relationship between religion, state and society in Turkey. In short, we focus on Turkish Islam by placing it in both its historical and its local contexts. From this perspective, we offer an answer to the question whether Turkish Islam constitutes an impediment to Turkish membership of the EU.

Limitations

We are aware that an assessment of the position of religion in Turkey is only one aspect of the considerations involved in Turkey's membership. No overall judgement is made in this Report. We will thus make no recommendation on the issue if, and when, membership negotiations should start. Such a recommendation requires a political judgement based on a close assessment of Turkey's progress with respect to all the Copenhagen criteria. In the autumn of 2004, this will be provided by a new report by the European Commission. Nor do we offer an opinion on the advantages and disadvantages of Turkish membership. Such an opinion would involve numerous other factors as the decision-making capacity of an enlarged EU, the geopolitical, economic and financial consequences of membership, the anticipated flows of migration etc., all important in themselves but all outside the framework of this report. What we do want to explore, however, is the question of Turkish EU membership in light of the growing international importance of political Islam since the 1970s. We will refer to this issue briefly, in the epilogue.

1.3   RESEARCH APPROACH AND STRUCTURE OF THE REPORT

The question whether the fact that the majority of the Turkish population is Muslim forms an impediment to EU membership, requires first a view of the Union itself. What is clear is that there exist widely divergent views on what the Union is and how it should develop in the future. Each viewpoint would apply different criteria to assess whether Turkey and Turkish Islam are consistent with EU membership. For example, those who see the Union as a community defined by Christian values, will employ different criteria in their assessment from those who view it as a union of culturally widely divergent states which take decisions jointly. For this reason, in chapter 2 we first present the Union's values as they have been developed in recent years by the member states themselves (section 2.2). The union is one based on shared values and objectives which grants rights to, and imposes obligations upon member states, and from which individual citizens also derive supplementary rights. The community of values rests not so much on a shared historical legacy of specific cultural-religious values, as on the minimum political and civic values institutionally anchored in the democratic constitutional state. These minimum values contain two crucial assumptions, relating to the position of religion in (future) member states: the separation of the state and religion and the guarantee of religious freedoms and rights. Defining exactly what this entails, is much less easy, given widely divergent relations between state, religion and society among member states. There is no agreed European standard that goes beyond these minimum values, and no model that the EU could offer Turkey (section 2.3).

Against this background, chapter 3 explores the core questions relevant for assessing Turkish Islam and Turkey as a Muslim country – how firmly rooted is the secular state in Turkey; how do Turkish Islam and the democratic constitutional state relate each to the other? Thus, the chapter starts with an exploration of the historical foundations of secular state (section 3.2). Next, separate thematic paragraphs investigate the current position of Turkish Islam in Turkey. One looks at the way in which the Turkish state has dealt with the rise of political islam (political movements based explicitly on Islamic principles) since the 1950s (section 3.3) and another examines the way in which Turkish State-Islam has dealt with freedom of religion (section 3.4). Finally, the chapter explores the relationship between political Islam and, in turn, democracy, human rights and violence (sections 3.5, 3.6, and 3.7 respectively). Chapter 4 will link these findings to the core question of the report and will formulate some final conclusions.

19

As indicated above, the subject of this report is in part dictated by the increased importance of political Islam world-wide since the 1970s. In this context, the question arises what influence Turkey's eventual EU membership could have on the Islamic world. Although this question is not central to the present report, we will return to it in the epilogue.

We have invited prof. dr. E.J. Zürcher, professor of Turkish languages and cultures, as part of this report to investigate the core question, also in light of the discussion on the 'clash of civilisations'. His results and the findings of the WRR are published together in this volume.

Text box 1.1   Turkey and Europe: recent chronology

1948: -Membership of the Organisation for European Economic Cooperation (OEEC)

1949: -Membership of the Council of Europe.

1952: -Membership of the North Atlantic Treaty Organisation (NATO).

1953: -Signing of a defensive Balkan Pact with Greece and Yugoslavia.

1954: -Signatory to the European Convention on Human Rights (ECHR).

1955: -Signing of the defensive Baghdad Pact with Iraq. Pakistan, England and Iran join later.

1959: -Discussions with the EEC on possible membership.

1963: -Signing of the association agreement with the EEC, which offered the prospect of membership after seventeen years.

1975: -Signing of the Helsinki Final Act establishing the Conference on Security and Co-operation in Europe (CSCE), precursor of the Organisation for Security and Co-operation in Europe (OSCE) founded in 1995.

1987: -EEC rejects Turkey's membership application, but offers the prospect of a customs union.

1995: -Associate member of the Western European Union (WEU). Signatory (together with eleven other Mediterranean non-member states) to the Barcelona Declaration on the Euro-Mediterranean Partnership.

1996: - Start of the customs union with the EU.

1999: -EU grants Turkey status of candidate member during the European Council of Helsinki. The Council concludes that Turkey must meet the same accession criteria as apply to other candidates, and that it will be eligible for pre-accession aid to support the reforms required for membership. The European Commission starts the preparations for a Partnership agreement for Turkey's accession.

2001: - Acceptance of the Accession Partnership and presentation by Turkey to the European Commission of the National Programme for the Adoption of the Acquis, in which Turkey's short and medium-term priorities are established, with a view to accession.

2002: - European Council of Copenhagen decides to grant membership to eight of the ten candidate member states from Central and Eastern Europe on 1 May 2004.
It decides that, "if the European Council decides, in 2004, on the basis of a report and a recommendation of the Commission, that Turkey fulfils the political criteria of Copenhagen, the European Union will commence accession negotiations with Turkey without delay."

2004: - Decision expected by the European Council in December, under Dutch EU Presidency, on whether to start accession negotiations.

NOTES

1   None of the official standpoints of the European Councils on Turkish
     accession, nor the regular reports which have been and continue to be
     composed by the European Commission on Turkey's progress towards
     the Copenhagen criteria, makes any mention of Islam. This comes as no
     surprise, since religion as such is not a part of the formal political criteria,
     which concentrate on constitutional and governance aspects of the
     member states. Representatives of the European Commission usually
     react to such inquiries by claiming that "our Heads of State and Govern-
     ment, the European Parliament, all official bodies of the European Union
     have always made absolutely clear that the European Union is based on
     common values, common principles and not on a particular culture or a
     particular religion" (quoted in the House of Commons 2001: 4).

2   One of the better-known and more recent statements in this vein was
     made by Valérie Giscard d'Estaing, the chairman of the now concluded
     European Convention for the drafting of a European constitution (which
     Turkey, incidentally, attended as an observer). At the end of 2002, he stated
     that an unbridgeable cultural divide existed between Turkey and Europe,
     that Turkey was not a European country and that its membership would
     bring about the end of the EU. He added that many European government
     leaders shared his standpoint, but dared not publicly to say so. Similar
     objections have been voiced earlier in the circles of the European People's
     Party (EVP) and the German Christian-Democratic parties, the CDU and
     CSU, and they were repeated recently in the context of the Convention. In
     their view, European cooperation is based on a system of common Chris-
     tian values, which has few points of contact with (Turkish) Islamic values.

3   The report presented to the European Parliament in May 2003 by the
     Committee on Foreign Affairs, Human Rights, Common Security and
     Defence Policy, compiled by Arie Oostlander, focused attention on the
     status of the religious minorities in Turkey. Oostlander, an MEP, expressed
     his concerns thus: "As a Protestant, I should have the same rights in the
     eastern Turkish town of Diyarbakir as a Muslim in Rotterdam. If this is not
     the case, and you still allow Turkey to become a member of the EU, then
     you're pulling the wool over our eyes" ('EU moet hard zijn voor Turkije',
     NRC Handelsblad, 11 February 2004. See also Oostlander's website:
     www.oostlander.net).

4   The terms 'secularism' and 'secular' evoke many associations, such as
     the decline in church membership, the disappearance of religion from
     the public realm, the banning by the state of religious expressions to the
     private domain and the (institutional) separation of church (religious
     groupings) and state. In this report, the term 'secular state' is employed to
     indicate that both the state's and the religious community's realms of

22

authority, remain autonomous. Secularisation is interpreted as a process in which the state acquires a greater autonomy in relation to the religious community.

2   THE EUROPEAN UNION AND RELIGION

2.1   INTRODUCTION

This chapter explores the main characteristics of the EU and examines how
the Union and its member states deal with religion. It observes that the EU
has evolved into a union of values and objectives that rests on the institutionally anchored political and civic values of the democratic constitutional
state, that guarantee the autonomy of church and state and religious freedoms and rights (section 2.2). After this, the chapter contains a brief survey
of the different ways in which the member states, both pro forma and de
facto, realise these basic values (section 2.3).

2.2   THE VALUES OF THE UNION

According to the Treaty of the European Union (TEU, article 49), "any
European state" may apply for EU membership. But what is 'European',
and what binds European states together? This question is increasingly
being asked now that the number of (potential) member states is growing
and the Union's list of tasks also grows longer (WRR 2003a). In its report
Towards a pan-European Union, the WRR concluded that geographical and
cultural-historical approaches often used to define Europe take insufficient
account of its dynamic and malleable nature. After all, Europe has a long
history of fragmentation, conflict and, especially, shifting political borders
that were all legitimised in various ways.[1] What remains is not a fixed
entity, but a dynamic social construct, an *imagined community* that can
change according to circumstance and political leadership (WRR 2001:
32-36). The developments of the 20th century confirm this. During the
1950s and 1960s the then political leaders of the 'Europe of the Six' saw
their experiences of destructive warfare and genocide as the foundation
for joint economic action. Since the end of the Cold War, the aims of tran-
scending national differences, and of consolidating peace, democracy and
prosperity, have certainly lost none of their relevance. However the
prospect of an EU of 25 members means that Europe is no longer seen as
synonymous with 'Western' Europe. Hence, most EU member states, as
well as the European Commission, have refrained from static cultural-religious, historical or geographical definitions of the Union. They recognise
that a degree of solidarity and some geographical limitation is essential for
communal action, without feeling the need for a blueprint with geographical borders or exclusionary non-universal values.

Realising that fundamental principles and objectives offer both grip and
flexibility, the EU typifies itself as an union of values and objectives (WRR

2001: 36). It is essential that (future) members subscribe to the fundamental principles, standards, rules and procedures of the Union (the union of values) and are also willing and able to pursue the concrete objectives of the Union (the union of objectives). In the treatment of candidate members this translates into a system of rights and obligations, in which the political-civic principles and values of the Union form the pre-essential conditions for membership. Only if these countries comply, may they submit a membership application. Both the Treaty of Maastricht (which became operational in November 1993) and the Treaty of Amsterdam (1 May 1999) extensively codify these principles and values. Article 6, par. 1, TEU, states:

"The Union is founded on the principles of liberty, democracy, respect for human rights and fundamental freedoms, and the rule of law, principles which are common to the Member States."

The European Convention on the future of Europe (2002-2003) stimulated further reflection on the normative foundations and points of departure of the Union, partly with the aim of bringing the European project closer to its citizens. The European Constitution, which was subsequently adopted by the heads of government in June 2004, underlines the importance of the union of values. The preamble states:

"Drawing inspiration from the cultural, religious and humanist inheritance of Europe, from which have developed the universal values of the inviolable and inalienable rights of the human person, democracy, equality, freedom and the rule of law,

Believing that Europe, reunited after bitter experiences, intends to continue along the path of civilisation, progress and prosperity, for the good of all its inhabitants, including the weakest and most deprived; that it wishes to remain a continent open to culture, learning and social progress; and that it wishes to deepen the democratic and transparent nature of its public life, and to strive for peace, justice and solidarity throughout the world" (Provisional consolidated version of the draft Treaty establishing a Constitution for Europe, 2004).

Article I-2 of the Treaty, entitled 'The Union's values' also states:

"The Union is founded on the values of respect for human dignity, liberty, democracy, equality, the rule of law and respect for human rights, including the rights of persons belonging to minorities. These values are common to the Member States in a society in which pluralism, non-discrimination, tolerance, justice, solidarity and equality between men and women prevail" (Provisional consolidated version of the draft Treaty establishing a Constitution for Europe, 2004).

The reference to religion in the preamble is the result of a debate on whether Christianity deserves to be mentioned explicitly. Instead of the existing reference to the 'cultural, religious and humanist inheritance' as a source of inspiration, some demanded the inclusion of a more explicit reference to the 'Judeo-Christian tradition'. Still others went even further by defining the current EU as a 'Christian community of values'. This would allow them to disqualify Turkey from membership in advance. The discussions in the Convention and the subsequent intergovernmental conference have convinced most participants in this debate that the value-question is a difficult one. After all, it would be strange if the member states of a Union based on *universal* values, would appeal to Christian values to deny a country membership. Moreover, it would conflict with their plea to cherish (religious) pluralism and diversity (article I-2 of the draft European constitution), and with the EU's efforts to bridge historical differences.

Religion is thus not included among the values on which the Union, according to the treaties and the draft constitution, rests. Naturally, religion does appear in the European Convention on Human Rights (ECHR), which is annexed to the new constitution. Article II-10-1 provides for freedom of thought, conscience, and religion, and article II-21-1 prohibits discrimination *inter alia* on grounds of religion or conviction. In addition, article II-22 states that the Union respects cultural, religious and linguistic diversity. Although these articles represent positive Union law, they do no more than define the minimum values and fundamental rights listed above.

The definition of the EU as a political-civic union of values and actions, based on "respect for human dignity, liberty, democracy, equality and respect for human rights, including the rights of persons belonging to minorities", prevents the use of cultural, religious or historical characteristics and values to exclude potential members. However, a consensus over basic values does not mean that exclusion, division or conflicts can always be avoided. Precisely in concrete situations there will always be disagreements and tensions over the hierarchy of values or their application (WRR 2003b: 47-53). Concrete judgements will always entail more refined considerations of what is valued, in which context, and in relation to which other values, by whom and for whom. This holds true whether the subject is the interactions among individuals, among groups or among member states. A good illustration of this is afforded by the 'conflict of values' between Austria and the other fourteen EU member states, that arose after

27

the 2000 electoral victory by the FPÖ, whose leader, Jörg Haider, had previously made decidedly negative comments about immigrants. When the ÖVP embarked on coalition negotiations with the FPÖ in January of that year, 'the fourteen' threatened to apply sanctions against Austria should the FPÖ enter government. They claimed that, by pressurising Austria to exclude the FPÖ from the government, they were attempting to protect the common values of the Union, as formulated in article 6, sect. 1. This action led to a deep crisis in the relationship between Austria and the EU. Neither the EU, nor any single member, had ever interfered so openly in the democratic process of a member state. Moreover, although the fourteen had justified their action by appealing to the values formulated in article 6, they could not implement sanctions on behalf of the European Union because, obviously, no concrete violation had as yet occurred. Once the FPÖ had joined the government, the fourteen jointly implemented bilateral sanctions. Austria reacted by threatening to obstruct the EU's decision-making process as far as possible and to hold a referendum on the sanctions. The stalemate was broken only after the EU Presidency, on behalf of the fourteen, asked a committee of 'wise men' to report on the attitude of the new Austrian government towards European values. The report concluded that Austrian immigration policy was compatible with the values of the Union, and argued that maintaining sanctions might have adverse effects.

The Austrian example demonstrates, first and foremost, that upholding certain values, even in the form of general legal principles, provides neither neutral nor unambiguous guidelines for concrete action. Second, the case demonstrates that procedures and the rules-of-the-game can contribute to the solution of differences of interpretation. The lesson, already learned earlier by the pragmatic EU, contributed to the decision to introduce into the Treaty of Nice (1 February 2003) a modification of article 7. This provides a more flexible and wait-and-see procedure when dealing with a "clear risk of a serious breach by a member state of the principles referred to in article 6, sect. 1".[2] Article 7 has already proved its worth. Although the new Italian coalition government, consisting of *Forza Italia, Alleanza Nazionale* and *Lega Nord*, that took office in 2001, again alarmed the EU, European leaders knew they were now backed by the new rules. This reduced the potential for rash actions or political crises, without jeopardising the exertion of peer-group pressure at the EU level on behalf of fundamental values.[3] Finally, the Austria case illustrates that, as the member states make greater demands on each other's constitutional democracies in the name of safeguarding common values, the battle against anti-democratic tendencies will require supplementary rules and mechanisms. These will become all the more necessary as fresh accession rounds simultaneously increase the diversity within the EU.

2.3 RELIGION IN THE EUROPEAN MEMBER STATES

2.3.1 MUTUAL AUTONOMY AND SAFEGUARDING FREEDOMS

Because, through political Copenhagen criterion, the European Commission evaluates the democratic state in Turkey, it also indirectly confronts the current members with questions and problems that had previously fallen outside 'normal' European political discourse and public debate. It asks questions as: what position should religion occupy in society? How should church and state relate to each other?

It is evident that present and future member states must have a democratic constitutional system that acknowledges and guarantees the autonomy of church and state and freedom of religion and conscience.[4] The principle that church (and religious communities) and state respect each other's autonomy has been laid down in national constitutions, in so-called concordats or agreements between the state and religious denominations, or has become embedded via the jurisprudence of national Constitutional Courts. The principle of autonomy implies that state and church each have separate domains of authority. Areas where the state has exclusive jurisdiction must be protected from direct interference by churches and religious communities. Conversely, the state has no direct authority over the internal affairs of the church and religious communities. None of this, however, prevents the state from requiring religious communities to observe the principles of the law. The fundamental right of the freedom of religion and conscience implies that followers of minority religions, atheists, and agnostics, by virtue of their beliefs, meet no restrictions in the exercise of their political and civil rights. This has legal implications both at the individual and the collective levels. The constitutional state should protect the individual from (group) coercion. The individual, however, may not, even for the sake of his (religious) conviction or affiliation, violate the fundamental principles of the state. The state must also realise the right to collective worship. Although these rights form part of the freedom of association and assembly and the freedom of expression, it is important that European states recognise the principle that these collective rights are open to all religious groups (Ferrari 2002:8). From this flows the principle of the neutrality of the state towards religion: the state may not favour one belief system over another. The political process, for example, must be equally accessible to persons of all persuasions. Contrary to what is often thought, this does not necessarily mean that faith and politics should be separated (Bielefeldt 2000:6; Rouvoet 2003).

In the case of Turkey's candidature, the European Commission criticises particularly the current situation of inadequate religious rights. The 2003 Regular Report concludes:

"Concerning freedom of religion, the changes introduced by the reform packages have not yet produced the desired effects. Executive bodies continue to adopt a very restrictive interpretation of the relevant provisions, so that religious freedom is subject to serious limitations as compared with European standards. This is particularly the case for the absence of legal personality, education and training of ecclesiastic personnel as well as full enjoyment of property rights of religious communities" (European Commission 2003).

Although these 'European standards' can be seen as referring to the principles of the freedom of religion embodied in the ECHR, there is no conformity among member states over how, in practice, this freedom and autonomy from the state should be effectuated. As will become obvious, this situation stems from the great diversity in national arrangements and, de facto, from the favouring of traditional religious communities within the member states. Moreover, the relationships between church and state, and religion and society remain highly sensitive in many member states (see also text box 2.1). Hence, in its assessment, the European Commission limits itself to applying only the minimum conditions.

2.3.2   A EUROPEAN MODEL?

To understand the actual role of religion in state and society, one needs to look beyond these minimum conditions which anyway are difficult to employ in practice. Equally, it is not enough to limit oneself to simple alternatives as whether or not there is a state church, whether or not there is religious pluralism, and whether or not the state subsidises religious communities. This will become even more evident when we abandon an exclusive focus on constitutionally and legally established relationships and embrace administrative, socio-political and cultural situations as well. As will be argued below, a varied and variegated approach makes it impossible to define one, ideal development path against which to measure the modernity of the Turkish state and of Turkish Islam.

The institutional autonomy of church and state in European countries today is the result of the Reformation, the processes of state-formation, the growth of modern capitalism and the modern scientific revolution (Bader 2003b: 57). The way in which those processes reinforced each other differed in time and place, and this created divergent path-dependencies. These, in their turn, were influenced by the success or the failure of the Reformation, which settled the divide between Protestant and Catholic/

Orthodox countries in Europe; by the extent to which the Reformation and the subsequent uprisings caused internal division (France, Belgium) or, conversely, unity in the face of an external enemy (the Netherlands against Spain; Ireland and the US against England); and, also by the presence or absence of an assertive, Enlightened critique of religion (such as existed in France and England, but not in Italy, Ireland and Spain) (see also text box 2.1).[5]

These different paths of development allow some general conclusions to be drawn on the evolution of the ties between state, church, religion, politics and society. First, it appears that although European states do indeed enjoy a considerable real autonomy of church and state, by no means have all states broken all official constitutional links with the church. Only the Netherlands, France and, until the fall of communism, most Central and Eastern European countries can be classified as states that have cut the constitutional ties between the dominant religion or church and the state (a process known as 'disestablishment').[6] England has a state church under the formal leadership of the head of state. The Prime Minister, via the head of state, appoints not only the head of the church (the Archbishop of Canterbury) but also the upper echelons of the Church of England. Places are reserved in the House of Lords for 26 senior bishops, in their function as 'Lords Spiritual', while six of the 33 officials charged with the management of church property are government civil servants. All these functionaries (including, by virtue of their office, the Prime Minister and the Minister of Sports and Culture) are accountable to parliament and to the General Synod of the Church of England.[7]

Over the course of time, countries such as Scotland, Norway, Denmark and Switzerland have replaced systems allowing for strong state domination over the church, with weaker constitutional links, but they have not entirely dispensed with their state church. Nonetheless, one cannot say that any of these countries are less democratic or modern. Second, the absence of a state church does not imply an absolute separation of church and state. In most countries where the state church was eventually abolished, or where it never existed in the first place, the de facto political and cultural domination by one church usually persisted, at least for a while. As a result, the mutual political and cultural influencing of religion, state and society generally continued (Bader 2003b: 59-61). For example, in countries such as Poland, Greece, Ireland, Bulgaria, Romania and Armenia, the ties between the state, the nation and the dominant church have remained extraordinarily strong. In the last three, the struggle for independence against the Ottoman and Turkish Muslims accentuated the ethnic significance of the church.

Text box 2.1   Christianity, church, state and nation in Europe

Struggles and schisms

The dominant and long-term presence of Christianity in Europe is still everywhere clearly visible. However, the Christian religion has not always been a binding, integrating and community-building force. The history of European Christianity is deeply scarred by conflicts between sectarian groups and movements (or groups without any formal church and/or hierarchy) and the established churches, principally the Roman Catholic, Protestant and Orthodox churches. These three major churches eventually each developed their own ties with the secular authority, thus obtaining legitimacy. At the same time, there played out a long struggle between the power centres of the state and the church. From about the 4th to the 19th century AD, representatives of the secular state authority all tended to lend direct or indirect support to a system in which one ('the true') version of Christianity enjoyed a religious monopoly. Religious uniformity and conformity, especially where it coincided with the territorial authority of the state, was considered to be in the interest of the state and its subjects and to reinforce internal order and stability. In this way, the state was supported and legitimised by the established religious authorities, which also benefited from the unity of doctrine and religious community. This found expression not only in laws based on religious principles, but also in the institutional entanglement of religion and state (Sunier 2004). When confronted with religious divisions among the populace (because of religious splinter groups, territorial shifts, migrations, etc.) the state in the early modern period usually reacted in one of three ways; either to suppress those opposing religious views which the church defined as 'heretical', or to distance itself from the established religious church order and shift towards the deviant religious community, or to tolerate (or ignore) deviant religious interpretations. Before the 19th century, complete religious tolerance, neutrality or complete suppression rarely occurred, probably because the Reformation had left a legacy of a deep-rooted fear of revolts and civil wars. It is notable that the multi-denominational countries of present-day Europe practice all these strategies, partially at any rate, including elements of suppression (as in the case of radical sectarian groups labelled as potentially violent, also towards the state). The legacy of conflicts between churches and sectarian groups, and the alternating struggles and cooperation among church, state and nation helps explain the sensitivity in many European countries of issues concerning church-state relations.

The legacy of schisms which have divided Europe into north, south, east and west is still apparent in post-1990 reunited Europe. The *World Christian Encyclopaedia* (2001) distinguishes cultural areas with zones where (combinations of) Roman Catholic, Anglican, Calvinist, Protestant, Lutheran, Orthodox, Armenian and Muslim communities live. The mono-denominational cultural zones, which include the Lutheran north, the Roman Catholic south and the Orthodox east, embrace over 406 million of the approximately 681 million European citizens (Madeley 2003).

Classifications

Numerous systems exist to classify the relation between church and state in the different European countries. Following Barrett et al., on the basis of formal legal criteria and perceived existing connections Madeley (2003) discerns three categories:
- states which promote (one) religion or religious institutions ('religious'),
- states which neither promote nor discourage religion ('secular'), and
- states which suppress religion ('atheist').

According to this classification, in 1980 no less than 22 of the in total 35 European states fell into the first category (the Vatican, Belgium, Denmark, Finland, West-Germany, Greece, Iceland, Liechtenstein, Luxemburg, Monaco, Norway, Spain, Sweden, Switzerland, Andorra, Portugal, England, Scotland, Italy, Malta, Ireland and Cyprus). Only five states fell into the second, secular group (Austria, the Netherlands, San Marino, France and Turkey) while nine were classified as 'atheist' (Yugoslavia, the former German Democratic Republic, Bulgaria, Hungary, Romania, Poland, Czechoslovakia, the USSR and Albania). However, most of the then communist states granted a special status to specific religious traditions, especially those considered historically closely associated with the nation-state. In Bulgaria, for example, even under communism a law continued to exist that stated: "The Bulgarian Orthodox Church is the traditional faith of the Bulgarian people. It is bound up with their history and, as such, its nature and its spirit can be considered a church of the popular democracy" (Madeley 2003). At the same time, however, the state and the communist party closely monitored religious institutions and activities.

A comparable classification of the relationship between church and state, undertaken in 2000 (covering a total 48 European states) found that 30 states belonged to the first category. This increase was due primarily to the 'transfer' of former communist countries and the recently independent states in Central and Eastern Europe from the category of 'atheist' to the other two categories. As a result, the secular category leapt from 5 to 17 states, whilst states justifying the catagorisation 'atheistic' disappeared entirely. Interestingly, the state control of religion in the latter countries was dismantled and, in most cases, made room for state support, either by means of financing the reconstruction or building of churches or by making public revenues available to recognised religious societies.

Religious communities, subsidiarity and EU decision-making

The growing significance of EU legislation increasingly attracts various philosophical movements, such as religious denominations and humanist organisations, into the Brussels political arena. This leads to the familiar pattern of 'Europeanisation' and mutual competition (WRR 2003a). On the one hand, many religious organisations attempt to safeguard their own national church-state model from European legislation, while on the other, they search out formal and informal methods to propagate their own, preferred (national), model at a European level, or at least to make sure, at that level, that people know they exist.

33

Formally, European institutions have no role in the relationship between church and state, since they fall under the so-called subsidiarity principle. This had already been established in the separate (not legally binding) Declaration 11 of the Treaty of Amsterdam, which states: "The European Union respects and does not prejudice the status under national law of churches and religious associations or communities in the Member States. The European Union equally respects the status of philosophical and non-confessional organisations" (European Union, Official Journal C 340 of 10 November 1997).

During the preparation of the Treaty, a *Commission of Experts of the Bishops' Conferences of the EU* (COMECE) and the *Church and Society Commission of the Council of European Churches* (CEC) failed in an attempt to include a statement to the effect that the particular model for church-state relations in each member state forms part of 'the own identity'. They were more successful, however, in getting Declaration 11 accepted into article I-51 of the new European constitution. Moreover, par. 3 added the provision: "Recognising their identity and their specific contribution, the Union shall maintain an open, transparent and regular dialogue with these churches and organisations" (Provisional consolidated version of the draft Treaty establishing a Constitution for Europe, 2004).

Informally, the most successful religious groups are either those that utilise so-called concordats (formulating special rights, social roles etc.) or those belonging to state churches or having for some time enjoyed recognition by a member state. The CEC and COMECE are, for example, are invited to the tripartite talks with the European Council that precede the half-yearly rotation of the European Presidency. Partly because of this and also because they maintain a staff in Brussels and are fed information from concordat countries like Germany, the CEC and COMECE have an advantage in ways and means over, for example, Islamic and humanist groups. The *European Humanistic Federation* has recently become more active in lobbying in Brussels and has employed some staff, while the Russian Orthodox Church and the Ukrainian Catholic Church opened offices in Brussels in 2002 and 2003, respectively. In addition to the European Council and member states, religious groups also engage in an informal, more diffuse dialogue with the European Commission and a six-monthly meeting with the Forward Studies Unit, the think tank of the president of the Commission. These dialogues allow for more space for other groups, as Muslims, Protestant minorities, Buddhists, Hindus, Scientologists, etc. (Massignon 2003).

Sociologists of religion have developed typologies of institutional and governmental arrangements, which enable a better understanding of the diverse patterns of relations between state, society and religion that have emerged over time. One typology, developed by Bader, identifies four dimensions of state intervention in religion:

1   the constitutional, legal, administrative, political and cultural links between church and state;
2   the goals of the state in religious questions;

3 the divergent powers (legislative, judiciary and executive) and administrative levels (federal, state, local);
4 the policy on areas other than those directly related to religion (Bader
2003b: 61-64).

The constitutional links concern the rules on religious freedoms and the
degree to which an established state church, with state obligations
embodied in a constitution, can be said to exist. These obligations may
include appointing or recognising church leaders, paying the salaries of
church officials and collecting taxes destined for the church. The legal and
administrative links range from the general but limited to the highly
specific but comprehensive, depending on the state's goals. States have
the ability alternatively to suppress, tolerate, protect or actively promote
(certain) religions and have a variety of political instruments at their
disposal (see text box 2.1). For example, most European states offer
special legal or administrative dispensations on the basis of religious
convictions. These include the right to refuse military service, the right to
discriminate against women and homosexuals on the grounds of religion,
and exemptions from Sunday trading laws and building regulations, etc.
They also often grant specific privileges, such as subsidies to religious
organisations, groups and schools. In brief, a state deals with religious
freedoms in different ways, which results in different balances between
competing interests of individual and collective religious autonomy, freedom and non-discrimination. Recent developments in immigration,
secularisation, individualisation and the emergence of new denominations, however, have all forced states to become increasingly pluralistic
and to search for new arrangements between state, society and religious
(minority) groups.

The formal constitutional or legal recognition by the state of a specific religion or religious community is no guarantee that its members can actually
establish themselves as a congregation – they may encounter local administrative or political hurdles. For example, in Belgium Islamic worship has
been recognised since 1974. A Royal Decree called for "...the institution of
(provincial) committees charged with managing the temporal affairs of
recognised Islamic communities" (Waardenburg 2001: 48). Because these
committees never got off the ground and because the Muslims themselves
long contested that state-recognised national body of Muslims as their
representative, actual recognition came only in 1998 in the form of
compulsory state funding of Muslim worship. Conversely, the absence of
formal constitutional or legal recognition does not necessarily mean that
actual institutional, political of cultural development is hindered. In the
Netherlands, for example, even after the 1983 constitutional changes
formally severing the financial ties between church and state, various

35

subsidy schemes for prayer areas and Muslim services were nevertheless established, within the framework of the country's integration policy. Since, formally, religious activities may not be subsidised, such subsidies are pragmatically labelled as social and cultural (Waardenburg 2001: 30; Sunier 2004). One exception to this rule is the right to special education, guaranteed in article 23 of the constitution, which protects state funding of religiously-based education. England does not even have a legal statute and, as a result, no church other than the Church of England can receive formal recognition or subsidies. Nevertheless, since the 1980s, many Islamic prayer-rooms have been registered as charitable organisations, enabling them to qualify for certain tax benefits. These charity benefits are also used by countless Islamic socio-cultural institutions and festivals. In England, however, the establishment of Islamic schools has encountered more problems than in the Netherlands because of greater local political resistance (Waardenburg 2001: 63-69).

In Germany, too, the institutionalisation of other religions sometimes encounters problems. In principle, the state views churches in a positive light, but it attempts to retain strict neutrality among different religions. Religious communities that have a permanent character and enjoy public-law status have the right, enshrined in the constitution, to a church tax imposed by the state. Moreover, the state can subsidise churches for social and cultural activities. Efforts by Muslim organisations to obtain this public-law status, however, have encountered great difficulties. In addition to the difficulty of proving that they are indeed representative (a problem also experienced in Belgium and the Netherlands), Muslim organisations also face political opposition on formal grounds. Some German authorities use the argument that Muslim migrants are by definition temporarily present in the country to deny the permanent character of Muslim organisations. Other opponents reason that Muslim discrimination against women is unconstitutional and, therefore, that formal recognition cannot be granted (Waardenburg 2001: 54-62). Even when the central government attempts to remain as neutral as possible, decisions involving privileges, subsidies, taxes, building permits, etc. will also usually, if indirectly, flow over into the political arena and influence political debate.

Using the four typologies described above, and taking the degree of religious pluralism into account, it is laicist France that best conforms to the pure model of separation of church and state.[8] As will become clear in chapter 3, notwithstanding some differences, there are interesting similarities between Turkish and French laicism. French laicism still has the scars of long and bitter conflicts between the state and its religious communities. Since the Middle Ages, Jews have endured pogroms and exile; in the 16th and 17th centuries, Protestants were persecuted and even expelled

(St. Bartholomew's Night and the Edict of Nantes, respectively), while, after the French Revolution, Catholics were severely persecuted as 'hereditary enemies of the Enlightenment'. The Congregation Act (1903) only recognised religious communities after they had applied for a compulsory licence, that had to be approved by the French parliament. The Jesuit Order refused to apply, on the grounds that God and not the French parliament constituted the highest authority. As a result, for many decades, Jesuit education was not offered in France. Since 1905, there has been legal, administrative, political and cultural separation of church and state and the state observes strict neutrality. Religious pluralism formally exists exclusively in the private sphere and the civic domain of *civil society*, not in the state. The latter guarantees freedom of religion and conscience and freedom to worship, formally without recognising, funding or subsidising religious services. There is, however, also a formal control-function entrusted to the Prime Minister, who (except in Alsace-Lorraine) has the right to propose cardinals and bishops, though the final appointment is left to the Vatican (Le Goff & Rémond 1992). Nevertheless, for decades now, France has been unable to avoid the de facto intrusion of pluralism into the public sphere, though the state has primarily accommodated it as part of its cultural policy.[9] With the influx of large groups of Muslims, however, the spectre of France's turbulent past has again surfaced. At the end of 2003, the so-called Stasi Commission recommended banning ostentatious religious symbols in public buildings. This move, though controversial, was supported by numerous, also religious, groups, who viewd this exercise of strict 'neutrality' as a safeguard for peace, order and religious freedom (Le Monde 12-12-2003). As one foreign commentator recently observed: "one must realize that a militantly secular and neutral French republic is perceived by most citizens as the only possible response to a long and tormented French past, rife with religious tragedy, a story in which Islam is simply the latest arrival" (*International Herald Tribune* 7-1-2004).[10]

Like France, Belgium, the Netherlands, Austria, and Germany have no state church, but unlike France, they do support religious pluralism in an administrative, political, cultural and, to a lesser extent, legal sense (for example, through family law). They recognise and encourage diverse religious organisations and try to draw them into the administrative, political and cultural domain, by means of (often decentralised) negotiations, the provision of information and the creation of advisory bodies. Norway, Denmark, Finland, England and Scotland combine a relatively weak state church with a limited degree of administrative, political and cultural pluralism. They do not accommodate pluralism, either in a fundamental or a legal sense, but instead employ a pragmatic approach to demands to institutionalise different religions. The new and candidate EU member states further increase the diversity of traditions and regulations in Europe.

Although their systems differ widely amongst themselves, in conformity with the political Copenhagen criterion, they have all enshrined freedom of religion in their constitutions. Even so, it is inevitable that, in practice, these countries afford a certain privileged treatment to the traditional religious communities. Several countries, including Bulgaria, Romania and Lithuania, go even further and exercise a deliberate policy to employ the dominant religion to bind and build the nation (U.S. Department of State 2002; Jubilee Campaign 2003).

2.4   CONCLUSION

According to the principles of the Treaties, the EU is a union founded on the political and civic values of the democratic constitutional state. It is emphatically not a union whose (potential) members subscribe to specific cultural-historical or religious values. All the same, its political-civic union of values assumes the existence of a state that guarantees the autonomy of church and state and protects general religious freedoms and rights. How this autonomy and protection are implemented, and the exact status of religion, varies widely in practice from country to country. The *real* position of religion in Europe, therefore, cannot easily be defined, whether employing the minimum conditions of 'the' secular European constitutional state, or employing the standard concepts of the still-popular modernisation theory. This theory suggests that all modern European states have followed more or less similar development trajectories, all of which resulted inevitably in the privatisation of faith, far-reaching secularisation and the complete separation of church and state. The reality is that European countries demonstrate divergent, historically determined relationships between religion, church, state and society, coupled with equally diverse legal, institutional and political arrangements.

What all this implies, is that there is no unambiguous, fixed European standard against which the current situation in Turkey can be measured. Nor are there any *a priori* reasons to assume that Turkey would, or would not conform with any of the available European development models. Furthermore none of these models and none of the situations are immutable. Changes, either endogenous or exogenous, as the arrival of new minority groups or the rise and decline of membership of different churches, will force the state to look again for a reasonable balance among the diverse interests and values that exist in a democratic constitutional state. For example, the state may have to reconsider the implications of the existence of a dominant religious majority for the opportunities for development of religious minorities. Similarly, freedom of conscience must be balanced against equal treatment and equal opportunities, and the need to protect the position of apostates must be weighed against the autonomy of the religious community. In short, there is every reason to examine the position of Turkish Islam from an historical perspective and to place it in the context of a dynamic equilibrium between state, politics and society. This will be the subject of the following chapter.

NOTES

1   A few examples may illustrate this. At the time of the Greco-Persian wars (5th century BC) the word 'Europe' regularly appeared as a territorial concept. It referred to an area to the north of the Greek states, inhabited by 'barbarians', and it was clearly distinguished from the Greek and 'Asiatic' Persian regions by language, customs and values (McCormick 2002: 31). On classical maps, the eastern border of Europe was delineated by the river Don. In the heyday of the Roman Empire (200 BC-400 AD) a large part of this 'Europe' was, for the first time, brought under a common administration, but the empire's centre of gravity lay in the region of the Mediterranean, including parts of North Africa and the Middle East.

2   The modified article 7 of the Treaty of Nice is as follows:

1   "On a reasoned proposal by one-third of the MS [member states], by the European Parliament or by the Commission, the Council, acting by a majority of four fifth of its members after obtaining the assent of the European Parliament, may determine that there is a clear risk of a serious breach by a Member State of the principles of liberty, democracy, respect for human rights and fundamental freedoms and the rule of law (Art. 6, par. 1 EU), and address appropriate recommendations to that State. Before making such a determination, the Council shall hear the MS in question and acting in accordance with the same procedure, may call on independent persons to submit within a reasonable time limit a report on the situation in the MS in question."

The Council regularly checks whether the motivations for its finding are still present.

2   The European Council, consisting of heads of state and government leaders, can, unanimously, acting on the proposal of one-third of the member states or of the Commission, and once the European Parliament has consented, diagnose a grave and ongoing violation of the principles stated in Article 6, par. 1, by a member state, after having requested the member state in question to submit its reactions.

3   When this has been determined, under paragraph 2, the Council, acting with a qualified majority, may suspend certain rights deriving from the application of this Treaty to the member state in question, including the voting rights of the representative of the government of that member state in the Council. In doing so, the Council shall take into account the possible consequences of such a suspension, upon the rights and obligations of natural and legal persons.

The obligations of the member state in question arising from the Treaty shall continue to be binding on that member state.

4   The Council, acting on a qualified majority, may decide subsequently to

modify or revoke measures taken through paragraph 3, in response to changes in the situation that led to their being imposed.

5 For the purposes of this article, the Council shall act without taking into account the vote of the member state in question. Abstentions by members present, either in person or represented, shall not prevent the adoption of decisions referred to in paragraph 2. A qualified majority is described as the same share of weighted votes of the members of the Council in question as laid down in article 205, par. 2, of the Treaty establishing the European Community.

This paragraph shall also apply in the event of voting rights being suspended pursuant to paragraph 3.

6 For the purposes of paragraphs 1 and 2, the European Parliament shall act by a two-thirds majority of the votes cast, representing a majority of its members."

3 However, it is a condition that the member states agree on what a 'serious breach' entails.

4 This also results from the obligations in article 9 of the European Convention on Human Rights (1951) in respect to freedom of thought, conscience and religion: "1. Everyone has the right to freedom of thought, conscience and religion; this right includes freedom to change his religion or belief and freedom, either alone or in community with others and in public or private, to manifest his religion or belief, in worship, teaching, practice and observance. 2. Freedom to manifest one's religion or beliefs shall be subject only to such limitations as are prescribed by law and are necessary in a democratic society in the interests of public safety, for the protection of public order, health or morals, or for the protection of the rights and freedoms of others" (European Union, Official Journal C 80 of 10 March 2001).

5 The outcomes of these four historical processes can be characterised, in line with Bader (2003b: 58), as: 1. complete monopoly: all Catholic or Orthodox member states; 2. duopoly or segmented pluralism: Protestant states with a substantial Catholic minority (60-40 per cent); 3. qualified pluralism: more pluralist; competition exists between the established church and a substantial group of 'dissident communities', both outside and inside the state church; 4. complete pluralism: full competition among all religious communities.

6 In the Netherlands, the very first parliament, the National Assembly, proclaimed in 1796: "We shall not tolerate any privileged or ruling Church in the Netherlands." The constitution of 1848 finally terminated the constitutional privileges of the Dutch Reformed Church and, in 1871, the Ministry of Worship was dissolved. A subsequent constitutional amendment in 1917 and the Education Act of 1920 granted a large measure of autonomy to religious communities. The 1983 constitutional reform severed the financial ties between the state and the churches (including the payment of religious functionaries) (Sunier 2004).

7   The extent of the legacy of the state church in England only became clear to most English in 2002. On the eve of Queen Elizabeth II's golden jubilee, *The Guardian* newspaper launched a campaign to repeal or amend the 1701 Act of Settlement, according to which only Protestant heirs of princess Sofia of Hanover could ascend the throne. Repealing this Act proved to be a complex matter, since it involved eight other, related, acts as well as the comparable legislation of at least 15 Commonwealth countries (Madeley, to be published).

That same year, a successor for the Archbishop of Canterbury also had to be found. According to law, the Prime Minister should appoint one of the two candidates nominated by the Crown Appointments Committee. The appointment itself is done by the Queen, who, in her capacity as head of the church, had sworn to uphold the Protestant state religion of England when she was crowned. Once elected, the Archbishop must take his place in the House of Lords alongside the other 25 bishops (the Lords Spiritual). England had only given the ECHR a legal basis in 1998, but this now implied that that the discrimination on grounds of religion embodied in the Act of Settlement was no longer legal. *The Guardian* described the Act of Settlement as "part of the complex web of arcane legislation that binds the monarch to and government with the Church of England," and saw the 1998 legislation as a possible step towards abolishing the state church. However, some bishops including the out-going Archbishop, called the state church "an essential bulwark of British society" (quoted in: Madeley, forthcoming). These examples of the entanglement of church and state could easily be considered somewhat eccentric expressions of the English love of tradition. However, elsewhere in Europe, the relationship between religious institutions, state and society – in all its variants – is also firmly on the political agenda.

8   The French Stasi Commission sees the concept of *laïcité* as based on three inextricably related values: freedom of conscience, equal rights in the spiritual and religious domain and neutrality of political power. In the words of the Commission: "L'égalité en droit prohibe toute discrimination ou contrainte et l'Etat ne privilégie aucune option. Enfin le pouvoir politique reconnaît ses limites en s'abstenant de toute immixtion dans le domaine spirituel ou religieux. La laïcité traduit ainsi une conception du bien commun. Pour que chaque citoyen puisse se reconnaître dans la République, elle soustrait le pouvoir politique à l'influence dominante de toute option spirituelle ou religieuse, afin de pouvoir vivre ensemble." See also: http://www.laic.info/Members/webmestre/ Folder.2003-09-11.4517/rapport-stasi.pdf.

9   As *associations culturelles*, for example, religious communities can enjoy certain tax benefits and qualify for subsidies (Waardenburg 2001: 71).

10   The conclusions of the Stasi Commission not only led to heated discussions in France, but also in other EU countries like the Netherlands. The

French embassy in The Hague felt this was sufficient reason to discuss the theme on its own website, under the title: "Debate about *laïcité*: Frequently Asked Questions."

3   TURKISH ISLAM AND THE EUROPEAN UNION

3.1   INTRODUCTION

Many arguments against Turkish EU membership assume that 'Islam' and 'Europe' are two different entities that are historically only distantly related. Such arguments usually see Muslims as a new group of postwar immigrants and their immediate descendants, who have increasingly appeared as adherents of Islamic fundamentalism. Such views embrace crude generalisations, in which the West and Islam are synonymous for separate civilisations that are basically incompatible. According to Samuel Huntington (1993, 1996), it is exactly between these two 'civilisation blocs' that armed conflicts will increasingly occur. His hypothesis confirms the characterisation of Muslims as a single group of traditional and possibly fundamentalist believers, antagonistic to the West. Islam appears as an antidemocratic religion, opposing, among other things, the separation of the state and religion. Muslims would like nothing better than to reverse this separation wherever it exists, and to introduce the *shari'a*, the Islamic law. From the perspective of this 'clash of civilisations', a Muslim country like Turkey can never be part of the EU, at whose core lie the values of democracy, respect for universal human rights and the rule of law.

45

This chapter examines how, since the founding of the modern state, Turkey has interpreted the secular democratic constitutional state, both formally and actually. It begins by examining how far the secular state is historically embedded in Turkey (section 3.2). It then explores how, since the 1950s, the Turkish state has dealt with the rise of explicitly Islamic political movements (section 3.3), as well as the attitude of Turkish state-Islam towards the freedom of religion (section 3.4). Finally, the chapter explores the relationship between, political Islam and, in turn, democracy, human rights and violence (sections 3.5, 3.6, and 3.7 respectively).

3.2   THE SECULAR STATE: HISTORICAL FOUNDATIONS

Historically, the area we now regard as Europe has virtually always been home to Muslims. There has been a century-long Muslim presence in Greece, and for long periods the Ottoman Empire occupied an area most people now regard as European territory. Europe's relationship with the Ottoman Empire, with present-day Turkey at its centre, was marked by long intervals of hostility and warfare. These form the basis of Europe's deep-rooted hostile image of Islam, an image that, incidentally, reinforced the construction of Europe's own identity (Zemni 2002). However, the relationship was equally marked by periods of mutual cooperation and reciprocal influence.

In many ways, the present Republic of Turkey serves as testament to this European influence, to which it has explicitly opened itself since the foundation of the modern state. Protecting the state from religious interference is pursued almost as rigorously in Turkey as it is in France, which reconfirmed its role as undisputed European champion of *laïcité* in the beginning of 2004 by banning 'ostentatious religious symbols' in public education. The French model of laicism, that completely insulates the institutions of the state from religious influence, served, to some extent, as a blueprint for Turkey, and this has often translated itself into similar standpoints, such as banning headscarves in government buildings and at public functions.

The protection of the state from religious influence is so strict, that the European Parliament has urged the Turkish government to adopt "a more relaxed attitude towards Islam and religion in general" in order to reduce intolerance and violent religious extremism (European Parliament 2003). Here indeed lies a paradox where the secular Union demands that the government of a Muslim country adopt a less laicist stance. The countering of religious influence on the state in Turkey, however, goes much further than it does in most EU member states. Indeed, secularism has gone so far that it appears as though Islam is subordinated to the state. It is almost the inverse of a theocratic state, where the public sphere is subordinated to the religious authority. Ironically, it is this theocratic model, currently practiced in Iran, which the West considers the primary problem of political Islam.

The present Turkish government, led by a party of Islamic persuasion, is strongly in favour of EU membership, not least because it sees the Union as a guarantor of the religious freedoms against the state and the army (see below). It supports the EU's demand for a more relaxed attitude towards Islam, but it has to tread cautiously. It has to take account of anti-Islam sentiments prevalent among EU citizens, and maybe also their governments, as well as those of the Turkish establishment, especially in the state apparatus, the military and the judiciary. The practice of the separation of state and religion, cherished by that establishment, goes back a long way. The secular character of the state also enjoys wide acceptance. However, as will be shown below, controversies especially over the social and political role of Islam still occur.

The so-called Kemalist state ideology of Turkey is based on the philosophies developed by Mustafa Kemal Pasja (later Atatürk), the first president of the Republic of Turkey (1923-1938). His ambition was to modernise the nation and, thereby, launch Turkey into mainstream Western culture. It was not that he was anti-Islam, but he viewed 'true Islam' as a rational and natural religion. Individual believers needed no mediation between man and God. Following this logic, Atatürk, viewed religious institutes as the caliphate (administration of the Muslim community) and the *ulema* (religious scholars) as obstacles to this end; he abolished the former and placed the latter under state control. Movements operating outside the state's control, such as the popular mystic Sufi orders, were prohibited. Family law, the only area of law at the time still based on the *sharia* , was abolished and reformed along the lines of the Swiss civil code. Constitutionally, Turkey became a secular state and Atatürk gave it a central role in the country's modernisation. After the Second World War, the military would increasingly usurp this role. The modernisation mission, which was resisted by parts of the population, also assumed the nature of a cultural offensive. This involved the banning of Islamic symbols, including the traditional headdress of women and men, from public life, and the closure of training centres for clergy and of the theological faculty.

In their study, Zürcher and Van der Linden point out that this secularisation did not begin in the 1920s with Atatürk. Rather, these reforms formed the conclusion of almost a century of secularisation of state institutions. Nor can we characterise the pre-reform situation as a theocracy, though that remained the ideal among Islamic legal scholars of the time. While still officially considered Islamic, in practice the Ottoman state had, of old, a secular administration. Moreover, the Islamic legal system itself had only a limited scope and was mainly concerned with family law and contract law. The administration of the vast Ottoman empire obviously required afar wider scope of legislation than this. The ulema's only task was to check that these other rules conformed to religious law. The ulema's main function, therefore, was to provide a religious legitimisation for policy. Islam was thus a cultural and political bridge between the state elite and the mass of the population. This double-sided nature of the Ottoman Empire, the decision-making autonomy of the sovereign and its religious legitimisation, sparked a modernisation movement already in the 19th century. After a series of setbacks, the state institutions were modernised on the European model, with new codes of law, new courts etc. France, in particular, served as a model, and these innovations were designed on laicist principles. The Ottoman Empire began to transmute into a modern state. Although modernisation was still accompanied by explicit references to religious law, in reality an elite emerged with a materialistic, scientific and secularised worldview.

In 1848, as elsewhere in Europe, the principle of the (divine) sovereignty of the ruler came into dispute. These controversies also involved the search for new forms of legitimacy, including nationalism ('Osmanism') and democracy (and citizenship). In 1876, the first constitution was agreed, and elections were held for the first Ottoman parliament, which guaranteed a proportional number of seats for the non-Muslims who comprised 40 per cent of the Empire's population. Incidentally, the timing of these developments towards democracy more or less mirrored that of large parts of Western Europe. The constitution made no mention of state religion, and although Islam-inspired arguments were used in parliamentary debates, the core message remained: democracy is inherent in Islam.

After the Ottoman defeat by Russia, the Berlin peace treaty (1878) required the Empire to relinquish territory, with the result that the share of the Muslim population in the remaining territory steadily increased. The earlier political liberalisation now faced an ideological backlash, designed to create a new identity among the Muslim citizens, and to add a new mystique and authority to the sultanate. This new nationalism, coloured with strong religious tints, mobilised Islam as a social cement and as a means of reinforcing state power. It resulted, under sultan Abdülhamit II (1876-1909), in far-reaching state intervention in the contents and propagation of religion. The state also assumed new responsibilities in education, communication and transport. Zürcher and Van der Linden see this period as extremely important in shaping views on the role of the state, which would later carry over into the creation of the Republic.

The revolution of 1908 by the 'Young Turks' witnessed the restoration of the constitution and parliament and the end of the sultanate. In substance, however, the national revival envisaged by the Young Turks represented a continuation of Abdülhamit II's ideology. It, too, aimed at enhanced state power, centralisation and standardisation, using the Islamic identity as a social cement for the population. This emphasis on Islam in the nationalist ideology was further reinforced by the Balkan war, in which the Ottoman Empire was attacked by four Christian Balkan states. The Young Turks propagated a modern Islam with an open attitude towards science; an Islam purged of the superstition of the Sufi sheiks and the conservatism of the ulema. Numerous measures were introduced to reduce the role of religious institutions in education, law and hospitals, and to replace these by increasing state control. Atatürk and his supporters belonged to the radical wing of the Young Turks. The Kemalist movement they developed, built on and advanced the programme of the Young Turks, and the founding of the Turkish Republic in 1923 gave them the opportunity to put these ideas into practice.

Until the Second World War, measures gradually promoting secularisation and efforts at state and nation building, were all imposed from above. They proved particularly popular among the urban population. However, the new power centres could not afford to ignore Islam. After all, Islam was embedded in the beliefs and vocabulary of an increasingly Muslim population (the consequence of territorial losses and population swaps after the Balkan Wars). Even so, it was always the needs of the state that controlled the institutional framework and determined the political role that Islam could or should play. This hierarchical and paternalistic ordering of society, and the enforced modernisation it enacted, found counterparts in Western Europe between the wars.

Samuel Huntington (1996: 91-3) characterises Turkey's assimilation of European (especially French) political ideas, such as the separation of spiritual and worldy power, as *borrowing*, thus implying that they lack depth and internalisation. In his eyes, such political institutions are alien to Turkey, and therefore less well-embedded than those in Western Europe. Our historical sketch above, however, observes that, on those issues essential for EU membership, there are important similarities with Europe, and sometimes almost parallel developments in Turkey and Europe. The fading power of the sovereign, the rolling back of the influence of religious institutions over the state, the changing forms of legitimising of the power centre, the continued influence of the legacy of the French Revolution and the Napoleonic era, the emergence of democracy – all these processes have also occurred in Turkey, not significantly later than in Western European states. It is true that Turkey copied much from Western Europe, from countries such as Switzerland, Belgium, Germany, Italy and especially from France (Koçak 2003). This is hardly surprising since Western Europe included most of the then world powers. Just as the United States today, so in the 19th century European powers formed the obvious points of reference. France was a major source of inspiration on constitutional questions for many countries, besides Turkey. The Netherlands, for example, based its own constitution on both German and French models and 'imitated' many French laws and institutions, and this 'borrowing' has not diminished their internalisation. The same applies equally to Turkey (see Zürcher and Van der Linden this volume).

49

3.3 SECULAR STATE AND POLITICAL ISLAM

After the Second World War, the Kemalist top-down model of cultural and political modernisation, in which Islam was marginalized as a reactionary bulwark, made way for a model that allowed more scope for bottom-up influence. Partly through fear of the communist Soviet Union and partly under American influence, in 1946 Turkey turned to the democratic path and introduced multi-party democracy. The many rural voters, barely touched by Kemalist modernisation, now became a relevant factor; so too did the opponents of Atatürk's authoritarian de-Islamization in political and public life (Erdoğan 1999). Initially this brought to power non-religious political parties, who were more tolerant towards Islam, and the government took steps to reintroduce Islamic education at schools, establish courses for preachers, allow the call to prayer to be made in Arabic, etc. These changes were viewed with great suspicion by the Kemalists and by the army, which after 1960 began increasingly to see itself as the guardian of Atatürk's legacy (Yesilkagit 1997). Heavily seeped in a faith in state sovereignty, they both had difficulty accepting the possible consequences of popular sovereignty. However, neither the non-religious Democratic Party nor its successor, the equally non-religious Justice Party, questioned the secular nature of the state control of mosques and muftis (advisors on matters of faith). Zürcher and Van der Linden suggest that the postwar period has seen two opposing interpretations of secularism: the Kemalist vision which saw secularism as a safeguard for freedom of thought against Islam, and a more neutral secularism that wanted to protect the state from religious influence, but expected the state to respect freedom of religion. In the words of Süleyman Demirel of the Justice Party: the state should be secular, but this does not mean that the individual should be as well.

Since the 1960s, a political movement has been emerging that is explicitly based on Islamic principles. This new phenomenon was not so much a reflection of greater piety as a result of socio-economic developments (Zürcher and Van der Linden, this volume). It is hardly a surprise that this movement appeared on the political stage as soon as the democratic system gave it the opportunity to do so (also see Erdoğan 1999). The movement, in which Necmettin Erbakan played a central role, articulated the ideals of small entrepreneurs and traditionally-minded citizens who, unlike the workers and industrialists, considered themselves unrepresented in the existing political spectrum. The Islamic elements of its political programme (the 'National Vision', or *Milli Görüş*) concentrated on strengthening ethics and morals in education and upbringing, fighting usury and corruption, abolishing articles in the constitution and criminal law that penalised the political use of religion, and freeing religion from state control. The Kemalist principle of equal rights for men and women – such as the voting rights for women, dating from 1934, and equal rights regarding education and employment – was left untouched. State secularism was accepted as the point of departure; freedom of conscience and expression were seen as the basis for democracy and human rights.

Like the other religiously-inspired parties, Erbakan's party was banned during the 1980 military coup. The establishment still harboured the notion that this more 'populist' Islam represented an anti-modernist and anti-secular force. The junta launched an ideological offensive to immunise the entire population against radical Islamic movements (those not controlled by the state) and to immunise the youth against socialism. The major tool in this offensive was Turkish nationalism; Islam was seen as only one component of the Turkish identity, though an important one. The junta had picked up some of its ideas from another movement, the 'Turk-ish-Islamic Synthesis', which was established in response to the leftist climate of the 1960s. In the period before 1995, this movement became very influential. Its supporters came from various conservative parties, particularly from the Nationalist Action Party which had a strong appeal among impoverished youth of the ghettos and which had also been banned in 1980. The ideological offensive stressed Turkish identity, unity and harmony, and military and authoritarian values. It presented Islam as an 'enlightened' religion, open towards science and technology. The Direc-torate of Religious Affairs, the *Diyanet*, was entrusted with protecting and propagating this state-Islam as central to Turkish national identity. Not surprisingly, following the coup, many adherents of the Turkish-Islamic Synthesis landed in important positions, especially in the educational and cultural sectors.

The Welfare Party, relaunched by Erbakan as an Islamic party in 1983, broke through in the elections of 1994 and 1995. Ironically, the Islamic politics of the junta itself probably prepared the path for its success. The party's supporters were found mainly among the local shopkeepers and traders, the affluent Anatolian entrepreneurial class of the provincial towns (whose numbers had grown rapidly as a result of economic liberalisation) and the migrants that moved to the big cities in ever-increasing numbers in the 1980s and 1990s. Because of the state's inability to offer these migrants essential services, they had to rely on private networks, particularly the mystic brotherhoods active in the cities, which were officially banned. A new military coup resulted in Erbakan's fall in 1997 and the outlawing of his party. The party resurfaced as the Virtue Party, but it had little success and fared badly in the 1999 elections before it was also banned in 2001. It almost immediately bounced back as the Felicity Party, with an extremely religious programme, a strong emphasis on conservative values and stan-dards and the intention to Islamise education. The party was soon split, however, because the younger members wanted far less emphasis on reli-gion and because a separate party might increase their chances of being accepted as a governing party by the military and other sectors of the state apparatus. It might also increase their acceptability to the voters, since various elections had shown a majority against a strongly religious programme. The new Justice and Development Party (AK Party), established in 2001, presented itself as a broad conservative party, with respect for Islamic values and standards but without an explicitly religious programme. The party won by such a large majority in 2002 that, for the first time since World War II, a single-party government was formed. The government was accepted by the military, although its work is still viewed with apprehension.

One noticeable aspect of the history of Turkish political parties is that even the Islamic political formations that shared the Turkish political landscape in recent decades also favoured the principle of separation of the state and religion, though they did advocate, and in the case of the current AK government allow, more freedom of religion than Kemalists would countenance. The confrontations between the state apparatus, including the army, on the one hand, and Islamic parties on the other, revolve around the two interpretations of secularism, mentioned above: one where the state has a *dominance* over religion and the other where both are *autonomous* domains on an equal footing. The separation of the state and religion is a broadly accepted facet of political life in Turkey, and its roots run deep, as deep as those in most EU member states. Thus, contrary to Huntington's assumption, Turkish secularism appears fully embedded. There is no reason for Europe to fear that political Islam aspires to placing religion above the state, and certainly not in Turkey. It is true that there are Turkish-Islamic movements in Turkey and other countries (Germany) that want to establish a theocracy, but their support-base is miniscule (see section 3.7). Europe's fears may well reflect more its own history of Christian ambitions towards the state. For example, the Roman-Catholic Church only decided to accept the principle of separation of church and state after the Second Vatican Council (1962-1965).

3.4   STATE-ISLAM AND FREEDOM OF RELIGION

Despite the formal separation of state and religion and the constitutionally guaranteed religious freedoms, the Turkish state, in practice, still exercises a strong control over religion. This is a legacy of the Ottoman period, although it reached its zenith in the heyday of Kemalism. Restrictions on, and state intervention in the content of religion go further than what is customary in EU member states. This explains why the EU is critically monitoring freedom of religion in Turkey.

However desirable greater freedom of religion may be, one needs also to consider the specific Turkish context. The incorporation of Turkish Islam by the state was accelerated on two occasions: in the early 1920s and in 1982. In the 1920s, the last vestiges of Islamic influence on the state were abolished with the dismantling the 'caliphate' and the *'seyhülislam'* (highest religious legal advisor). The latter was replaced by the Diyanet, with wide-ranging powers over religious life, including managing mosques, appointing preachers, offering instruction on the content of sermons and suppressing brotherhoods etc. This made possible the secularisation of the law and paved the way to a 'popular edification' focusing on modern Islam. The 1980 military coup must be placed against the backdrop of the international rise of fundamentalism, which the establishment feared might spill over into Muslim Turkey. Islamic political parties were abolished, and in 1982 the Diyanet was constitutionally entrusted with the task of protecting Turkish national identity. To counter undesirable Islamic influences, it was to propagate the 'correct', Sunni, Islam through the mosques and compulsory classes on Islam, with a strong emphasis on ethics, human rights and each citizen's duties towards state and country.

From the current European perspective, these measures are indeed somewhat excessive. This also applies to the ban on Erbakan's Welfare Party in 1998 (upheld, incidentally, by the European Court of Human Rights). Even so, other European countries in the postwar period have also sometimes considered banning parties (usually communist, racist or fascist parties) that they considered a threat to democracy and the constitutional state. Moreover, nothwithstanding the formal separation of church and state, EU states also maintain privileged relations with respect to both finance and content with certain denominations (see chapter 2) though none went so far as the Diyanet. Nor, in the EU, is freedom of religion unlimited; fear of sects, for example, occasionally results in a ban or refusal to grant a licence.

As described in chapter 2, the dogma of separation of church and state permitted existing arrangements between the two to continue, though their content differed from state to state, as did legal restrictions on the freedom of religion. Turkey is, therefore, no exception in its desire to protect its constitutional characteristics. One must concede, however, that it is exceptional that state organs co-determine the content of the religious message; the messengers themselves – the imams – are also civil servants. Even in European states where a state church exists, such as the Anglican Church in England and the Presbyterian Church in Scotland, it still remains an autonomous institution with respect to content. In Sunni Islam, which is the dominant religion in Turkey, there is no institution comparable to a church. The Diyanet could be seen, therefore, as its functional equivalent in the sense that administering religious personnel and effects is an important function. Equally, although Turkey also goes further than Europe in ensuring the 'correctness' of religious education, it should be remembered that European states also maintain some controls, though in the form of a tie between the cash flow and the (legal) conditions for receiving it. This

53

can be supervised, because the religious communities in question are legally accountable bodies. The absence of a similar institutionalised position of religion in Turkey, means that there are no such bodies to which powers and responsibilities can be transferred. In Sunni Islam, without a body such as the Diyanet, every mosque would be fully autonomous in practice.

The Diyanet includes representatives of traditional Islam and the more modern Sunni Islam. One consequence is that the state-Islam that is propagated by mosques and schools remains sufficiently flexible and realistic to offer a safe middle path, but that it does not exactly radiate renewal. The resulting message is a mixed appeal of social conservatism, human rights and freedoms, patriotism and obedience to the state. From the state's perspective, it is a safe message that is guaranteed by its institutional position. Similar safety is attained in Europe by tying church institutions that lie outside its domain, to both various conditions and to statutory supervision. The historically determined links between the Diyanet and the state have not served to prevent the emergence of alternative expressions of Islam. The educational activities of the *Süleymancis* and the *Fethullahcilar* are a good example of this. This plurality in practice has not yet been formally recognised.

Given the increasing freedom of religion and the emergence of Islamic political parties, it is no surprise that the Diyanet's position has come under discussion. This discussion has naturally spilled over onto the compulsory education in state-Islam and ethics at school, and the favouring of certain denominations. Various participants have urged the state to adopt a more neutral stance towards religion. The smaller *Özgürlük ve Demokrasi Partisi*, for example, has questioned the constitutional position of the Diyanet, and was disbanded for its pains (Koçak 2004). It is very difficult for the state apparatus to countenance changing the status of the Diyanet, since it represents an important instrument in the control of Islam. However, the incident has led to a decision, following a ruling of the Constitutional Court, to scrap the legal provision for disbanding a party on the grounds that it had challenged the position of the Diyanet (Koçak 2004).

Turkey's EU membership would confront the Union with a state whose historical development has left it with ties between religion and the state that go further than those of any other member. This relationship is unlikely to change much in the short term, but the longer term is a different matter. As democratisation advances in Turkey, it will contribute to the formal recognition of greater social plurality, including religious plurality. This, in its turn, will have implications for the way in which the state intervenes in religion, and possibly even for the position of the Diyanet. As demonstrated by Zürcher and Van der Linden's account of the so-called 'pocket catechism', part of the message is that Islam requires obedience to the state. Further democratisation will undermine this Islamic legitimacy for a strong state, and to contest state actions will be regarded as a normal phenomenon. Democratisation will mean that society will acquire more influence over the state through the political arena. This would allow the Islam advanced by the Diyanet to aquire a more civil and individual character. The Diyanet might even offer its facilities to other Islamic movements and religions, giving it a new position, and one more independent of state power.

3.5 DEMOCRACY AND POLITICAL ISLAM

It is not only the issue of the separation of religion and the state that fuels the doubts in the EU on Turkish membership; the EU is also concerned about the relationship of Islam to democracy in general. Turkey's postwar political history has been a turbulent one, and this is obviously not what the Union is waiting for. The interventions of 1960, 1971, 1980 and 1997 were all targeted at the manifestations of political Islam at the time. Political Islam has clearly been an explosive factor in Turkish politics. But were these Islamic parties a danger for democracy? Did they want to overthrow democracy, or were they, on the contrary, manifestations of democracy?

As we have already shown, none of the successive Islamic political parties has ever wanted to attack the secular character of the state. However, they have advocated a different type of secularism than that contained in Kemalist state ideology. Kemalist politicians considered the very existence of religion as an attack on the foundations of the Turkish Republic. Islamic political parties, by contrast, viewed democracy as based on freedom of conscience, expression, religion and religious practice. None of them has ever contested the value of democracy in their programmes and they have always worked within the rules of the democratic constitutional state to exert their influence. For example, Erbakan did not fight the banishment of his Welfare Party in 1998 on the streets in the name of Allah, but in the European Court of Human Rights (see Zürcher and Van der Linden). He also accepted its decision that the ban was lawful. This suggests that the problem of Turkey is not the antidemocratic or anti-human rights nature of political Islam, but rather, the state's fear of the consequences of democracy (Yavuz 2003).

From the moment of political Islam's emergence in the 1960s, it has polarised the political debate in Turkey. Given the Turkish state's history of denying and suppressing Islam as a political force, this is not surprising. The Islamic-political breakthrough, both locally and nationally, during the

55

1980s and 1990s, kept the temperature high on the issue, as did interna-tional developments in the form of the rise of Muslim fundamentalism and terrorism. However, the extreme reactions in Turkey against political Islam were not justified by events on the ground. The political manifestation of Islam, through its various mutations in Erbakan's party, expressed the wishes of groups that did not identify with the Kemalist project. This drew new demographic groups into the public arena and into politics. This mani-festation was also an outcome of major socio-economic changes that were taking place in Turkish society, including the emergence of a new middle class, stimulated by economic liberalisation, and large-scale migration to big cities. Since the Islamic parties were based largely on regional and local organisations and networks, they in fact helped create a political sector that was far more representative of society as a whole (Yavuz 2003: 227-231). Despite many disagreements with the establishment, some recent, Islam as a politically relevant factor has gradually become accepted in Turkish poli-tics. This suggests that extending the 'normal' political channels and broadening the political arena may have had a 'pacifying' influence on the debate.

Islamic parties initially stressed religion and focused on the Middle East and Central Asia. In this they were reacting against the secularist basis and European inspiration of the Kemalist movement. Yet, according to Yavuz, there was a remarkable reversal in the following decade in attitudes towards Europe and the EU. Whilst part of the state establishment began to see the EU as a threat to Kemalist nationalism, supporters of political Islam began to appreciate a difference between the Kemalism and the EU. They now overwhelmingly support EU membership, convinced that the Union offers a form of secularism that sees freedom of religion as a fundamental human right, and one to be protected. The plea of European institutions for democratisation and respect for human rights in Turkey has played an important part in this transformation (Yavuz 2003: 254-261).

This reversal in perspective, however, does not mean that the prospect of EU membership will actually simultaneously strengthen the hands of anti-modernist forces. There are several reasons for this. Firstly, both the Kemalists and political Islamists in Turkey have been greatly influenced by modern European ideas and practices (Yavuz 2003: 265-274). Secondly, Turkey has never been a colony. Unlike Islam elsewhere in the Muslim world, Islam in Turkey never became an ideological vehicle for nationalist resistance to a Western oppressor. The Western influences present in Turkey are the result of the country's own choices and not of coercion by foreign powers. Whilst many changes have been imposed from above by its own elite, they remain indigenous products. The West is portrayed as an enemy to Islam to a far lesser degree than in other Muslim countries. If there was indeed a Western enemy, it was Russia and later the Soviet Union. This resulted in Turkey's membership of the NATO, which constituted the joint Turkish-European-Atlantic military framework for the fight against communism. Communism was also political Islam's greatest enemy. Thirdly, it also missed out on large-scale socio-economic deprivation and frustration that formed a breeding-ground for extremism elsewhere in the Muslim world. Fourthly, unlike some other Muslim countries, any existing dissatisfaction could always manifest itself through politics, and government parties and could always be voted out of office. This is also why political Islam in Turkey lacks the extremist characteristics that can be found elsewhere. There have been fifteen national elections since World War II, of which twelve were free and fair (see Zürcher and Van der Linden). Fifthly, Turkey's climate of moderation is also attributable in part to the rapidly growing urban middle class, who share religious beliefs (and also demand that they be recognised by Kemalists) but who are also the children of eighty years of secularism and Kemalism. Sixthly, despite being formally banned, the Sufi movements and their intellectuals have had an important influence on Turkish Muslims and have contributed to the fact that pluralism and moderation are important features of Turkish Islam. Finally, Turkish Islam's traditional orientation towards the state allowed it to develop a pragmatic and flexible character.

We have already referred to the headscarf affairs in both Turkey and European states in recent decades. The gradual recognition of Islam as a socially and politically relevant factor was accompanied by an awareness among well-educated young people that Islam is part of their identity. These people certainly do not wear headscarves as a display of traditionalism or an expression of fundamentalism. They seek recognition of their Muslim identity through this symbol, in particular in the public domain, which had been so long, and so explicitly, ideologically closed to them (Göle 1996). Zürcher and Van der Linden suggest that this recognition is founded not in theology, but in an appeal to human rights (in this case, the individual right to show one's religious conviction). Basically, the breakthrough of political Islam has ended the distinction, cherished in the Kemalist discourse, between 'modern Kemalists' and 'backward Muslims' (Yavuz 2003). The fact that the current Islamic inspired government recently proposed a bill against discrimination of homosexuals and got it through Parliament (The Economist 21-2-2004), does not fit with the usual image of Muslims held in the West. In short, the state has lost its ideological monopoly on modernity. If the state apparatus, including the military, gains more respect for democracy and recognises the autonomy of civil society, the differences that existed for so long between state and society may eventually disappear.

Zürcher and Van der Linden rightly stress that one should avoid the impression that religion is the single most important issue in Turkey, or in a discussion on Turkish democracy. Their study and ours, which both focus on religion, could easily create this impression. However, it is not true that the increasing role of political Islam and its electoral success are determined solely by religion. Turkish voters do show some religious preferences, but they, too, would vote out religious parties from government that would fail to meet their expectations on, for instance, economic performance or the fight against crime and terrorism. Moreover, the Turkish electorate seems to prefer moderate parties; and moderate in an Islamic sense as well. When, for example, in the last elections in 2002, it had a choice between the more outspoken Islamic Felicity Party and the moderate AK Party, the AK Party won by an overwhelming majority, even in the constituency of Erbakan, the leader of the Felicity Party.

Surveys show that the Turkish population characterises itself as being largely religious, but certainly not religiously zealous; as being tolerant and not at all fundamentalist. The majority is opposed to religion playing a role in political life, supports the secular character of the Republic and also thinks that the state should stay out of religion. They see religion as part of the private area and strongly dislike the exploitation of religious differences (Çarkoğlu and Toprak 2000). The 2002 Eurobarometer also shows that the majority of the Turkish population favours accession to the EU. The proportion in favour is higher than that of all the (then) candidate states. This fervour is relatively untouched with knowledge, but levels of knowledge on the EU are low among other candidates as well, not to mention within the EU itself (European Commission 2002).

3.6   CONSTITUTIONAL STATE AND POLITICAL ISLAM

As indicated in section 3.2, the current law in Turkey is secular law. Koçak (2004) divides the history of the legal system into three periods, with 1839 and 1920 as cut-off points. Islamic law persisted formally in the Ottoman period until 1839, alongside a large body of secular law, sanctioned by the Islamic authorities. After 1839 the Islamic state made room for a state with a mixed legal system. For example, the Criminal Code of 1858 (a translation of the French code of law of 1810) banned most traditional *sharia* punishments. Incidentally, the stoning of adulteresses had already been abolished in the seventeenth century. The commercial law that was introduced in 1850, which was also derived from France, permitted the charging of interest, a financial concept contrary to the *sharia*. During this period there were separate secular and Islamic courts, as well as mixed courts, each covering different legal areas. By and large the influence of the religious courts diminished. Of all areas, family law remained under Islamic law the

longest, but even that was abolished in 1917. With the foundation of the
Republic of Turkey, the last remnants of legal pluralism were removed. The
sharia courts were forbidden in 1924, and in 1926 a new civil code of law
was introduced, based on the Swiss model. The wearing of religious dress
in government buildings was prohibited in 1925. The Criminal Code of
1926 prohibited the use of religion for political purposes, and in 1928, the
still existing article that referred to Islam as the state religion was removed
from the constitution; a new preamble identified national sovereignty with
a laicist and democratic republic (Koçak 2004).

This long history of legal secularisation, which had been inspired by the
legal systems of several European states, is indicative of how embedded
this law is in the country. Legal secularisation was no innovation of the
Kemalist movement, but had gradually taken shape over a long period
when the country was an Islamic state (see also Zürcher and Van der
Linden). Moreover, the many steps in this process were always freely
taken, in contrast with elsewhere in the Muslim world, where they were
imposed by a colonial power, or assumed in order to please the West
(Koçak, 2004). This also means that the secular law has become an endogenous feature of Turkey. It may well be more endogenous than even the
Turkish establishment realises, with its forced reactions against any alleged
breaches of the secular character of the state. While the participation of
Islamic parties in elections is evidence that the law against the use of religion for political purposes has been superseded, incidents like the headscarf affairs are still highly controversial. The position of the Diyanet,
which now falls directly under the Prime Minister, is also highly sensitive,
and any discussions on the subject can quickly be considered to overstep
the boundaries of political debate permitted in the constitution.

59

The Refah Party was banned in 1997 by the Turkish Constitutional Court.
The banning itself was not based on Refah's party programme (which actually subscribed to the secular state), nor on its actions in government. It
was based on a number of separate actions by officials (such as wearing a
headscarf, advocating the possibility of prayers during working hours) and
a few speeches by its leader, Necmettin Erbakan, in which he demanded the
right of believers to live under their own legal system (sharia) and linked a
fair social order to jihad.[1] The Constitutional Court insisted that this boiled
down to advocating legal pluralism, and undermining the secular character
of the state.

The ban was subsequently upheld by the European Court of Human
Rights, but on the basis of statements of individual party officials, and not
on the basis of an official party programme. However, it is worth noting
that the Court tested their statements against the constitution that had

been introduced in 1980 by the military junta, and also that the Court was much divided. A minority saw no compelling or convincing evidence in the official actions of the Refah Party, either that it wanted to destroy the secular order, or that it promoted violence or religious hatred (Koçak 2004).

Erbakan's appeals at his party's conferences for reintroducing elements of the sharia says nothing about the electoral popularity of the issue. For example, according to sociological surveys quoted in the previous section, an overwhelming majority rejects the reintroduction of the religious law into family law (such as recognition of Islamic marriage or divorce) and only 10-15 per cent are in favour (Carkoglu & Toprak 2000).

Although the principles of the secular rule of law have a strong basis in Turkish history and current society, this says nothing about attitudes towards human rights and their enforcement. This issue is extremely important in assessing whether Turkey meets the Copenhagen criteria, and the progress in this field is justifiably a major topic in the regular reports of the European Commission. This test will not be carried out here, but the attitude of Turkish political Islam towards human rights is obviously an important point for attention.

It is remarkable that political Islam demands a place in political space by appealing to human rights. Zürcher and Van der Linden argue that democracy and human rights are applied as a reference framework, because this is an accepted discourse in the Turkish situation. After all, EU membership is supported by Islamists (the supporters of political Islam), because the EU would offer a better protection of freedom of religion than the Kemalist state. This raises the question how far the appeal to human rights is inspired by self-interest – creating a legal room for oneself – rather than a recognition of the rights of others. In his 1975 book, also quoted by Zürcher and Van der Linden, Erbakan states that his movement is loyal to all rights and freedoms enshrined in the constitution. All the same, he saw the Turkish system as one allowing non-believers to deny human rights to believers. Erbakan wanted the stipulation in criminal law that penalises the political use of religion replaced by a Human Rights Protection Act. This would suggest that his appeal to human rights was indeed largely inspired by the need to safeguard the rights of believers and of his own political movement. Seeing how controversial freedom of religion was for Kemalists and how much opposition Erbakan's various Islamic parties generated, this is not so surprising.

The current governing AK Party is much more explicit on the universal implications of human rights. Its election programme pays much attention to the issue and proposes many modifications to bring Turkish law and practice in line with European norms. It sees differences in religion, culture and opinion as an enrichment of society, and considers secularism as one principle of freedom which makes this plurality possible. It proposes that people with a different language, religion, race and social status must be able to express themselves freely on the basis of equal legal protection and, as such, must also be able to participate in politics. The programme also explicitly discusses the equal rights of non-believers. It clarifies that all these objectives, and the measures to implement them, are not a means of obtaining an entry ticket to the EU, but are necessary for the country's modernisation. Its success will require a change in the relationship between state and society; a change whereby the current authoritarian *top-down* approach makes way for a state at the service of society.

This approach is more sensitive to the positive value of plurality, including religious plurality, than that advocated by the state and even perhaps that offered by the Refah Party. The AK Party's perception of human rights is an inclusive one and not a particularistic concept to enhance its own electoral chances. The European Commission's reports will reveal in due course whether, now it is in government, the AK Party acts in the same spirit. The 2003 report records that great progress had been made (European Commission 2003). Making allowance for the usual rhetoric of election programmes, the Party's intentions do not appear to be solely based on political opportunism. Its views reflect long-term changes in Turkey. Socio-economic transformations and improved education have both contributed to a broadening of the political space; a broadening from which Erbakan's parties have especially benefited. As was the case with its predecessors, the current AK Party is also supported by local and regional networks of activists who unify – often divergent – aspirations under the symbolic flag of Islam (White 2002). In the Kemalist climate, Islam could only obtain grudging recognition as a political force through regular confrontations. However, this broadened the opportunity for the public debate, and the state was seen less and less as automatically right. After the confrontations of the 1980s and 1990s, the AK Party made full use of this opportunity and has synthesised and consolidated its message. The earlier polarisation between Islamism and the Kemalist movement has disappeared from its election programmes and has been replaced by a very strong focus on the constitutional state. It now accepts the state must be subjugated to the law, the state should be neutral towards religion, it should advance democratisation and guarantee 'inclusive' human rights in which the freedom of expression occupies a central, strategic place. This will allow the party to overcome electoral differences between Islamists and Kemalists.

61

The conditions for the new social contract between state and society now seem to be present. At the same time, freeing the reins for democracy to flourish in Turkey, will not happen without resistance.

3.7   VIOLENCE AND POLITICAL ISLAM

A special concern in EU member states is whether Turkey's membership will introduce religious-nationalist or religious-based extremism and violence into the Union. It is true that religious violence is no stranger to some member states, as shown in the long conflict between Protestants and Catholics in Northern Ireland. The same applies to the nationalist violence that is still part of the independence struggle of the Basques in Spain. In both cases, the conflict remained largely within local or national frontiers. However, because of the large number of Turks in different member states, an outbreak of violence in Turkey would possibly quickly spill over its national frontiers.

One can distinguish three ideal-type positions in Turkey's current political-religious landscape: modernism, traditionalism and fundamentalism. Modernists are open to a continuous reinterpretation of the moral ideal, as revealed to Mohammed (see Zürcher and Van der Linden) They emphasise the moral independence of the individual and his freedom and ability to gain relevant moral knowledge for changing conditions. While traditionalists also allow an interpretation of the moral ideal, when it has taken place and been ratified by believers, it cannot be revised. As a result, the authoritative text of Islam is increasingly expanded with the interpretations of previous generations. The fundamentalists, however, oppose the right and the necessity of subjective interpretation and ascribe an absolute meaning to the original texts and sources. They want to model social and political life according to the Muslim community at the time of Mohammed, and introduce the *sharia*. This is often motivated by the wish to protect the moral ideal against manipulation and corruption by rulers.

Mainstream Turkish Islam relates to modernism and traditionalism. Modernism, which views Islam primarily as a personal religious conviction and is open to science, can be found among the Young Turks, in the subsequent Kemalist interpretations of Islam, as well as in major branches of the *Nurcu* movement. The National Vision (*Milli Görüş*), and *Nakşibendi* movement from which it originates, can be considered to be part of traditionalism. Fundamentalism does not have to be violent, and this is shown in some of the *Nurcu* movements, such as the *Aczmendi's*, but also within the Milli Görüş movement. Violent fundamentalist movements are of course illegal. It involves a small number of numerically limited but very active movements. These include the banned group 'Islamic Great Eastern

Raiders- Front' (IBDA-C), which refuses to recognise the Turkish state and wants to heal the divisions in the Islamic world. It rejects the European influence on Turkey and wants it replaced by Islam, not only as a religion, but also as a civilisation. It has a clandestine branch that does not shun violence, that possibly maintains contacts with al-Qaeda, and that is suspected of being responsible for the suicide attacks in Istanbul in November 2003. Another movement is *Hizbullah*, whose aim it is to establish an independent Islamic state. In the 1990s it also used terror against the Kurdish PKK and progressive Turkish and Kurdish businessmen and intellectuals who sympathised with their cause. It has been claimed that this movement was used by security forces in the fight against the PKK. When the security forces no longer needed them, it was largely disbanded. The 'Caliphate of Cologne', a prohibited splinter group of the National Vision movement, also wants to overthrow the secular state and democracy in Turkey, and it has proclaimed the caliphate from Germany. The movement has recently been banned in Germany, but its activities continue underground.

These underground movements are not averse to using violence to realise 'holy' aims in Turkey, such as the founding of an Islamic state absorbing Turkey into a broad Islamic framework and introducing the *sharia*. Their aims are not only diametrically opposite to those of the Kemalists, but they also represent a break with a tradition going back to Ottoman times, since when a tradition of a separation of religion and state existed in practice. Given the long history of the secular state, and its support by the mainstream of Turkish Islam and most of the population, it would seem that the realisation of these aims is illusory. The more relaxed attitude of the state towards Turkish Islam and, in particular, its political manifestations, as is advocated by the European Parliament, could perhaps reduce even further the following of these extremist movements.

63

Underground movements would view Turkey's accession to the EU as the highpoint of betrayal. It is therefore far from inconceivable that, in the run-up to EU membership, violence will intensify, perhaps also in the current member states. The EU should not allow this prospect to change its position on Turkish membership. To do so, would imply that these small groups of extremists and terrorists could hold the country to ransom and sabotage the membership ambitions, cherished and supported for so long by a broad cross-section of the population.

3.8   CONCLUSION

Not only are there differences among current EU member states in the
development of the formal and practical relationship between the state and
religion, so there are between EU member states and Turkey. Nevertheless,
especially in developments of importance for the secular, democratic
constitutional state, the historical development of Turkey has many parallels with that of Europe. Although officially Islamic, the Ottoman state
for a long time had a secular state system, and the range of Islamic law
remained restricted largely to family law and contract law. Both the
Ottoman state, and later the Turkish state, were formed by a combination
of the crumbling power of the sovereign ruler, the declining influence of
religious institutions, the changing grounds for legitimacy of the power
centre, the continued effect of the legacy of the French Revolution and
Napoleonic period, the influence of constitutional innovations elsewhere
in Europe, and rising democracy. Against the background of the emerging
democratisation of the 1960s, there emerged alongside existing social and
cultural movements, political parties that were more explicitly based on
values inspired by Islam, and that demanded greater freedom from the
state. This enabled the goals both of greater religious autonomy *from the
state* and of firmer guarantees of religious freedoms *by the state*, to gain
increased and broader support. These beliefs, which are consistent with the
EU requirements for the democratic constitutional state, have become an
important motivation for the supporters of the current Turkish government to strive for their country's membership of the EU.

NOTE

1   Jihad means 'striving' or 'struggle'. It is, however, a concept which has
     many different, context-dependent meanings, both in the Islamic world
     and beyond. Many feel that a distinction should be drawn between 'great
     jihad', the internal, mental struggle of the believer to do right, and the
     'small jihad', the armed struggle on behalf of the faith and the community
     of faithful. Others view jihad primarily as the struggle for (social) justice.

4 CONCLUSIONS

The EU has committed itself to assessing Turkey's membership using the same procedures it applies, and has applied, to other candidate member states. Although the religion-factor plays only a limited role in this assessment, it is precisely this factor that has generated so much disquiet. This is why, through this report and the supplementary survey, the WRR has attempted to contribute to a greater insight into the characteristics of Turkish Islam and the historical background of its relationship with the Turkish state.

The central question posed in this report is whether the fact that the majority of its population is Muslim will be an obstacle to Turkey's accession to the EU. The answer is negative. Neither the historical developments described, nor the characteristics of present-day Turkey and Turkish Islam, could justify the argument that Turkish Islam forms an obstacle to Turkey's accession to the EU. The WRR has reached this conclusion by also taking into account the widely divergent ways in which the present member states of the Union realize the relationship between state and religion, both formally and actually.

67

That fact that Turkey is a country with a predominantly Muslim population, certainly presents the EU with a unique situation. After all, the Christian faith is the dominant religion in the present member states as well as in the other candidate countries. So religion, i.e. Islam, has understandably become a talking point. In the supplementary study, Zürcher and Van der Linden highlight the paradox that it is precisely the EU member states, with their discourse on the separation of church and state, which include the substance of the religion in their assessment of Turkish membership. An additional factor explaining concern over Turkey is the general perception of Islam, including the rise of political Islam in Muslim states and also, naturally, recent manifestations of religious-inspired terrorism. This has contributed to the idea that the Islamic world and the West are incompatible, and that the Islamic worldview has no room for the attributes of Western democratic constitutional states; it is said to favour establishing the state on theocratic, as opposed to democratic, principles. This would mean dissolving the separation of the state and religion, replacing secular law with its Islamic counterpart, and recognising Islamic rights only, rather than a more universal concept of human rights.

Islam, like Christianity, has many faces. As far as Christianity is concerned, there are considerable differences, both within and between countries and regions, and the development of the relationship between church and state varies from country to country (see chapter 2). This is a generally accepted fact in Europe, but far less is known about the different manifestations of Islam. Consequently, there is a tendency to consider and discuss Islam in terms of generalities. However, the pluriformity that so characterises Christianity is also found in Islam. Turkish Islam has its own, unique characteristics and its extensive plurality is largely determined by Turkish history and context. This is also true of the political manifestations of Islam in Turkey.

Turkish history has in some respects a striking number of parallels with that of Western Europe. On the subject of the separation of the spiritual and the worldly domains, the development of the secular constitutional state and also the early manifestations of democracy, its history reveals even a considerable simultaneity. For its constitutional and legal development, Turkey has looked to Europe for models long before even the founding of the Republic. This historical development had meant that values and institutions important to the EU's assessment of Turkey's membership are firmly embedded in Turkish society. The principles of the democratic constitutional state are also shared by the mainstream of Islamic political philosophy in Turkey that has existed since the 1960s. There are no grounds for suggesting, therefore, that Turkey does not share the cultural heritage on which the EU is based. Modern Turkey is characterised by a state system in which Islam has no say and the state actually controls Islam. Freedom of religion therefore, forms a major demand of Islamic political parties. The law and the legal system are based on the same secular principles as those of EU member states.

Chapter 3 showed that Turkey has experienced distinct periods of serious polarisation between the state apparatus on the one hand, and society on the other. The two most sensitive issues have always been Kurdish independence and the social and political role of Islam. Given the fact that it took centuries to reduce the boundaries of the Ottoman Empire to those of modern Turkey and to transform a religious state to a secular one, it is not surprising that these territorial and religious sensitivities exist. It is surprising, however, that the country went through this substantial reduction of its territory and change in character without being seriously affected by Muslim extremism and without losing its principal focus on Europe. These processes have left it with a reasonably well-functioning democracy. While the global revival of Islamic activism in the 1970s and 1980s did not leave the country undisturbed, it did not deflect it from its pro-EU and democratisation course. On the contrary, it gave rise to an Islamic political movement that forcefully embraces this course.

Like every candidate country, Turkey also has its problems. For example, the Kemalist state philosophy, which sees political Islam as an anomaly, has been cherished and vigorously defended by the state system until this very day. From the EU's perspective, this state orientation forms a greater problem than does the rise of political Islam. The attachment to a strong state has prevented the realisation of a fully-fledged democratisation of society, although Turkey undoubtedly has a form of controlled democracy. The state supervision on the political process is still a sign of the fear of Islam as a political force, and it led to tight restrictions on its expressions.

This role of the state and, more especially, of the military, is obviously unacceptable if Turkey wants to join the EU. Both the European Commission and the Parliament are, therefore, right to demand that the military be placed under civil control, a demand also made to Central and Eastern European countries. Recent developments have been very promising, including the reform programmes and planned change of the constitution, developed with one eye to accession. Nevertheless, the WRR points out that the normalisation of the relationship between the military and the civil administration should take account of its impact in advancing the democratic process. Could the withdrawal of this 'guardian' of the secular government and the secular state contribute to such a resurgence of Muslim fundamentalism, that it might challenge the advances already made? And what if Turkey were, at that moment, already a member of the EU?

69

The long history of democratic and constitutional state institutions testifies to their entrenchment and their stability in present-day Turkey. It would, however, be a sign of historicism on this basis to claim certainty about the future. The fact that something has existed for a long time, is no guarantee that it will continue to do so. However, while taking this into account, it still is possible to formulate some expectations.

In the first place, the WRR considers the chance of an attack on the democratic rule of law to be remote because of the broad popular support for membership of the Union, a dislike among Turks of religious intolerance and the sociological processes (described in the previous chapter) that form the basis of political Islam. As section 3.6 shows, the electorate has regularly expressed its preference for moderate parties and appears to have abandoned a more radical Islamic phase, support for which was anyway always limited. The purifying effect of democracy applies just as much to Turkey as to other countries. From a sociological standpoint, the preference for moderation is not only an expression of ideas, but also of interests; and the large middle class has a great economic interest in accession to the EU. Likewise, advocates of a greater freedom of religion also view accession as an important protection of this religious freedom.

In the second place, membership of the Union may even have a mitigating effect on the tensions within Turkish society. Since 1961, the military has always committed itself to upholding security in Turkey; it often regarded political manifestations of Islam as a threat to that security. In other words: using state-Islam to hold mosques to a conservative-nationalist philosophy, has retarded the development of a more liberal Islam and prevented an open religious-social dialogue.

Christian-Democratic parties are a normal phenomenon within the political landscape of member states and this should also apply to Islamic-democratic parties. Integration into a secular Union that has committed itself to safeguarding rights and freedoms (and that will focus even more on this if its new constitution is ratified) will allow Turks to create more space for Islamic parties and make them a more acceptable phenomenon. The socialisation implied in the acceptance of 'rules-of-the-game' involved in EU membership, will mean that the role of the military will shrink by itself.

Nonetheless, it is not impossible that both the military's weakening grip on the democratic and administrative process, and the loss of sovereignty that EU membership implies, will initially play into the hand of traditionalist and nationalist political movements. In countries in Middle and Eastern Europe, where the transfer to democracy was even more sudden, this process was indeed initially accompanied by such a radicalisation. On the other hand, a truly democratic political arena will also allow liberal-Islamic (counter)forces to mobilise, which, in the past, have always been pushed to the background by the conservative state-Islam.

Even if it is initially accompanied by considerably fierce debates, the growth of a flourishing plurality does not have to be assessed negatively. Rather, it should be seen as a necessary condition to realise a better balance between state, religion and society. For example, the current government, supported by the women's movement, has led the attack both on the formal and actual discrimination against women and girls, and on the still frequent use of violence (honour killings) against them. This subject has been taboo until now, also because those involved justified 'traditional behaviour' by referring to Islam. These traditions, however, are not restricted to Muslims; they can also be found in Christian Mediterranean countries (AIV 1999: 14). As long as the legislation and its implementation comply with the ECHR, the EU has few other grounds for calling the Turkish state to account for these wrongful practices. It is all the more important, therefore, that the Islamic aspects of these practices are debated in Turkey itself and – as is happening now – that Muslims themselves condemn these practises. Those of the opinion that Islam orders these practices will obviously also speak out. This, too, is important. After all, the Union is not competent to decide on what is Islamic and what is not. Only the Turks themselves, with the support of the law, can end these culturally-determined practices. However, neither Turkey nor any EU member in the same position should have the illusion that such practices will end in the foreseeable future. For the EU, and for Turkish minorities in EU states, it is very important that the government and Islamic authorities in Turkey itself send out clear signals that discrimination of women and honour killings have little to do with Islam, and that the latter are also criminal. That the taboo on this issue has been broken in Turkey, is a positive development. A further democratisation will have comparable effects on other issues that are still considered taboo.

Various arguments can be given for the expectation that the secular democratic rule of law in Turkey will not be endangered should its self-proclaimed 'guardians' withdraw, though the gradually increase in freedom will initially result in a much broader range of opinions, and create greater contrasts than exist in the current controlled democracy. The period between starting accession negotiations and the actual accession itself may still take many years, but nonetheless it offers Turkey the chance gradually to become further accustomed to European practices. Once Turkey's accession becomes a fact, one cannot exclude the possibility that new situations may arise that will threaten the democratic constitutional state, for example a renewed coup. This danger, however, does not only apply to Turkey. Since many of the new member states have only recently converted to democracy, the danger has certainly not become smaller. As indicated in chapter 2, the Union has proved in earlier conflicts that it is able to formulate rules to handle this. New types of conflicts may force it to do this again. The previously agreed procedure applies in the event of a "clear risk of a serious breach by a Member State of the principles referred to in article 6, par. 1" (see chapter 2). Should the Turkish government have to deal with strong anti-EU forces due to certain developments, the constitution of the Union provides for the possibility of voluntary withdrawal (art. I-59).

71

The WRR considers it unlikely that these procedures, designed for situations in which the paths of Turkey and the EU may fundamentally diverge, will be needed. Nevertheless, they reduce the risk of mutual damage should the union not succeed.

On the basis of these considerations on the future, we feel there are no grounds for the assumption that Turkish Islam forms an impediment to membership. We therefore recommend that, should the government share this view, it should actively propagate it at home and abroad.

EPILOGUE

The WRR does not consider that the characteristics of Turkish Islam as such constitute any obstacle to EU accession. Yet, if the Turkish accession becomes reality, will it not also be important for the relationship between the West and the Muslim world? This relationship has become increasingly problematic, for example through spiralling Islamic terror and invasions of Afghanistan and Iraq. Could Turkish accession temper the fear of an unavoidable 'clash of civilisations'?

It is obvious that this should not be the main reason for allowing Turkey to join the EU. Accession should be judged on its own merits, on the basis of the criterion of an adequate functioning EU as a union of values and objectives. No-one will profit from a watered-down Union. However, if Turkish membership is accepted, this issue would become very relevant. For governments whose populations currently oppose a Turkish membership, this could be an important additional argument in its favour. The EU does not only want to maintain an internal legitimacy and effectiveness but, since it cannot isolate itself from the world, it also has a great interest in peaceful external relations. Now that the composition of the population of the EU is increasingly reflecting the world population, internal relations are also no longer immune to discordant relations elsewhere.

As indicated in chapter 2, the historical rationale of the European integration project was not to create a link among nations with a similar identity and culture or with equal values and standards. Nor was it a project among states with a mutual history of peace. It all began by supranational partnership and economic integration to end a history of conflict among countries that displayed great differences of identity, culture, values and standards. Looking at the situation today, and at existing animosities, one could legitimately ask whether the European integration project can again play a role in defusing conflict.

In the world today, the relationship between the West and Islam is unambiguously problematic. In the early 1990s, Samuel Huntington (1993) already argued that there would be new conflicts after the Cold War, in particular between these two civilisations. Since then, this 'clash of civilisations' has been accepted by many parties in Islam and in Western countries as a characterisation of the relationship between Islam and the West. The attacks of 11 September 2001 and subsequent wars and new attacks seem to confirm that it is correct. As stated in chapter 1, the recent hesitations of member states towards Turkey's EU candidacy are partly based on this kind of analysis.

73

According to Zürcher and Van der Linden, Turkey's membership would be a hopeful sign for the Islamic world that the West does not support the paradigm of 'clash of civilisations', as many Islamic countries had thought and feared. Perhaps, too, Western achievements could also find a place in Muslim countries. The WRR shares this opinion. In general, Turkish membership indicates that the two worlds are not mutually exclusive. Should Turkey become part of the Union, it will put an end to the idea of two geographically distinctive blocs, each defined by religion. As a result, at least one condition for maintaining the clash paradigm would become unsustainable. Zürcher and Van der Linden also demonstrate convincingly that the concept of greatly divergent civilisation blocs is untenable from an historical and cultural viewpoint. There is actually far more similarity between, and simultaneity in, developments of Turkey and Europe than allowed for in Huntington's concept. The many Muslims in EU member states also mean that the European identity and civilisation can no longer be defined in purely Western terms, and perhaps this has never been the case. Should Turkey be refused EU membership on *religious* grounds, it would be a signal to these Muslims that they can only belong to Europe by becoming totally assimilated. Conversely, Turkey's accession would emphasise that they already fully belong to the Union.

It is more doubtful whether, as a member of the Union, Turkey can function as a model for other Muslim countries. The arrangements existing in Turkey are determined by highly specific historical factors that are absent in other Muslim countries. Moreover, the Arab world sees Turkey as a former coloniser and as a current accomplice of the West. Taspinar (2003) therefore describes the Turkish situation as *sui generis* instead of as a model. He points to the authoritarian nature of the Kemalist movement and the role of the military, to argue it is not yet possible to speak of a fully-fledged liberal democracy. Together these factors will prevent Turkey from becoming a model, though it may still exercise a more general influence. In a dynamic sense, Turkey could certainly be an inspiration for other states, because it shows that Islam and democracy are not necessarily incompatible. Eventual EU membership will benefit Turkey by further embedding democracy and protecting rights and freedoms. Moreover, there will be a greater pressure in the Arab nations for increased democratisation and more respect for human rights. The two recently published *Arab Human Development Reports* of the United Nations Development Programme (2002 and 2003), in addition to '9-11' and subsequent wars, have reinforced the internal pressure on this front. For many Muslim governments, Islamic extremism is a nightmare, as a result of which there is a greater fear of democratisation and of offering citizens more protection against the state.

The recent relatively large openness of the Turkish political system to the different expressions of political Islam has protected the country against the degree of extremism that occurred elsewhere. Democracy was not introduced with a big bang, but gradually, and under the cautious and suspicious 'guidance' by the military. Whatever people think about this role, and however harshly it was enforced, the army always withdrew to their barracks shortly after intervening. In this respect, the Turkish development also differs from that of many other Muslim countries (Taspinar 2003). A report by the British Parliamentary Commission for Foreign Affairs on the accession of Turkey to the EU refers to this special position of the Turkish military. After all, since 1961, the military has had the constitutional task to protect the security of Turkey against domestic as well as foreign enemies. As such, it enjoys a great trust among the population. Although it does not see the role played by the military in defining and controlling the boundaries of the democratic process as entirely negative, this British Commission condemns the military for overestimating the dangers by political Islam to stability and the secular nature of the state. While it sees the present position of the Turkish military as unacceptable for the EU, the Commission urges that reforming its constitutional and social position be taken very seriously and that a way be found to gradually place it under civil control (House of Commons 2001). On the subject democratisation, Zakaria also refers to the importance of gradualness. Liberal democracies do not start on demand. Experience shows that if their introduction is too swift, the chances are high that this will result in 'illiberal' democracies. He considers that constitutional liberalism – separation of powers, the constitutional state and protection of basic liberties – should precede democracy: if power is not first limited, its execution may degenerate into tyranny, however democratically the power might have been obtained (Zakaria 1997). Through internal and/or external pressure, many Muslim states still have to follow the path towards a further democratisation, and have to avoid the risks described by Zakaria. At the moment, these countries are less stable than Turkey, and the Turkish experiences in gradually loosening the military's grip on society could be very instructive.

75

The Turkish record on human rights and freedoms is definitely not unblemished. According to Graham Fuller (2003), its authoritarian secularism can certainly not be applied as a model for other countries. Despite this, however, Turkey shows that political parties have gradually been given a place in the political spectrum that does justice to their own Islamic traditions and the growing democratic participation of the population. This Turkish development took place by trial and error, but it has eventually offered a learning curve showing how the secular state, democracy and political Islam can be brought into line with each other within one constitutional framework, albeit with some stick-and-carrot from the EU in the form of prospective membership. This may encourage countries wishing to follow the same path, to experiment with the rule of law and democratisation themselves. Turkey does not offer them any model; rather, it is a laboratory in which experiments take place that are interesting for other countries (Yavuz 2003: 7).

In many Muslim countries there are distorted views of the West, and vice versa. Some views need correcting. It is not true that Western secularism involves the hostility of the state towards religion in general and Islam in particular. It is not opposed to religion and it does not endorse nihilism, immorality and lawlessness. This also applies to Western views on the backwardness of Islam, and the anti-democratic and intolerant character of its followers. The 'discovery' by Islamic parties in Turkey, in contrast to earlier held prejudices, that the EU guarantees their freedom to manoeuvre, is a major step forward. As a member of the Union, Turkey, which has been in the forefront of debates on Islam, and is already well acquainted with the idiom of the debate, could certainly have a bridging function in correction misperceptions on both sides, and soften the contours of a debate that is still too often cast in terms of incompatibility and an inevitable 'clash'. To the conclusion that the characteristics of Turkish Islam do not stand in the way of Turkey's EU accession, one might add the rider that membership might smooth the growing differences (and perceptions thereof) between the West and the Islamic world.

LITERATURE

Adviesraad Internationale Vraagstukken (1999) *Naar rustiger vaarwater. Een advies over de betrekkingen tussen Turkije en de Europese Unie,* 9 July.

AK Parti (1999) *Development and Democratization. Program.* http://www.akparti.org.tr/programeng3.asp.

Bader, V. (2003a) 'Religious diversity and democratic institutional pluralism', *Political Theory,* 31, 2, 265-294.

Bader, V. (2003b) 'Religions and states. A new typology and a plea for non-constitutional pluralism', *Ethical Theory and Moral Practice* 6, 55-91.

Bielefeldt, H. (2000) *Moslims in de lekenstaat. Het recht van moslims mee vorm te geven aan de Europese samenleving, deel I en II.* http://www.flwi.ugent.be/cie/CIE/ bielefeldt10_a.htm#noot.

Çarkoğlu, A., and B. Toprak (2000) *Religion, Society and Politics in Turkey, 2000. Summary report of survey results.*

Economist, The 'Turkish women. Thou shalt not kill', 21 February 2004.

Erdoğan, M. (1999) 'Islam in Turkish Politics. Turkey's Quest for Democracy without Islam', *Critique,* 15, 25-50.

European Commission (2002) *Candidate Countries Eurobarometer 2002, First Results,* Directorate-General Press and Communications, http://europa.eu.int/ comm/public_opinion/archives/cceb/2002/cceb_2002_highlights_en.pdf.

European Commission (2003) *Regular Report on Turkey's progress towards accession 2003,* Brussels.

European Convention (2003) *Draft Treaty establishing a Constitution for Europe,* Luxemburg: European Communities.

European Parliament (2003) *Report on Turkey's application for membership of the Euopean Union,* Committee on Foreign Affairs, Human Rights, Common Security and Defence Policy, (COM(2002) 700 – C5-0104/2000 – 2000/ 2014(COS)) A5-0160/2003, 20 May.

European Union (1997) *Official Journal C340 of 10 November 1997, Treaty of Amsterdam,* http://europa.ev.int/eur-lex/en/search/treaties_other.html.

European Union (2001) *Official Journal C80 of 10 March 2001, Treaty of Nice,* http://europa.ev.int/eur-lex/en/search/search_treaties.html.

Ferrari, S. (2002) 'Islam and the Western European Model of Church and State Relations', 6-19 in: W.A. Shadid & P.S. van Koningsveld (eds.), *Religious Freedom and the Neutrality of the State: the Position of Islam and the European Union,* Leuven: Peeters.

Fuller, G. E. (2003) *The Future of Political Islam,* New York: Palgrave Macmillan.

Goff, J. le & R. Rémond (1992) *Histoire de la France religieuse, Tome IV,* Paris: Seuil.

Göle, N. (1996) *The Forbidden Modern. Civilization and Veiling,* Ann Arbor: The University of Michigan Press.

House of Commons (2001) *Turkey,* Select Committee on Foreign Affairs, Sixth

report, http://www.publications.parliament.uk/pa/cm200102/cmselect/
cmfaff/606/60603.htm

Huntington, S. (1993) 'The Clash of Civilizations?', *Foreign Affairs*, 72, 3, 22-49.

Huntington, S. (1996) *The Clash of Civilizations and the Remaking of the World Order*,
New York: Simon and Schuster.

International Herald Tribune, 'The long bloody path that led to French secularism',
7 January 2004.

Jubilee Campaign (2003) *Religious Freedom in new and future* EU *member states. Law
and practice*, http://www.forum18.org/PDF/EUaccession.pdf

Koçak, M. (2004) 'The Clash of Civilizations': Turkey (forthcoming 2004).

Madeley, J. (2003) 'A Framework for the Comparative Analysis of Church-State Relations in Europe: North and South, East and West' in: idem (ed.), *Religion and
Politics: Europe*, Ashgate: Dartmouth Press.

Madeley, J. (forthcoming) 'European Liberal Democracy and the Principle of State
Religious Neutrality' in: Z. Enyedi & J. Madeley (eds.), *Church and State in
Contemporary Europe: The Chimera of Neutrality*, London: Frank Cass.

Massignon, B. (2003) *Regulation of religious diversity by the institutions of the
European Union: from confrontation of national exceptions to the emergence
of a European model.http://hirr.hartsem.edu/sociology/sociology_online_
articles_massignon.html*

McCormick, J. (2002) *Understanding the European Union. A concise introduction*,
London: MacMillan.

Monde, Le 'Document. Le rapport de la Commission Stasi sur la Laïcité', 12 December
2003. See also: http://www.laic.info/Members/webmestre/Folder.2003-
09-11.4517/rapport-stasi.pdf.

NRC *Handelsblad*, 'EU moet hard zijn voor Turkije', 11 februari 2004.

Provisional consolidated version of the draft Treaty establishing a Constitution for
Europe, CIG 86/04, 25 June 2004.

Rouvoet, A. (2003) *Scheiding van kerk en staat is geen scheiding van geloof en politiek*.
http://www.tweedekamer.christenunie.nl/nieuws.php?tekstId+=333

Sunier, T. (2003) 'Scheiding van kerk en staat?', *GroenLinks Magazine*, 2

Taspinar, O. (2003) *An Uneven Fit? The 'Turkish Model' and the Arab World*, The
Saban Center for Middle East Policy at the Brookings Institution, Analysis
Paper 5, Washington D.C.

Toprak, B. (2001) *Religion and the state in Turkey*.
http://www.dayan.org/mel/toprak.pdf.

Trouw 'Turkije niet aan het lijntje houden', 2 February 2004.

United Nations Development Programme (2002) *Arab Human Development Report
2002. Creating Opportunities for Future Generations*, New York: UNDP.

United Nations Development Programme (2002) *Arab Human Development Report
2003. Building a Knowledge Society*, New York: UNDP.

U.S. Department of State, Bureau of Democracy, Human Rights, and Labor, *International Religious Freedom Report 2002*,
http://www.state.gov/g/drl/rls/irf/2002/ 13986.htm.

Waardenburg, J.D.J. (2001) *Institutionele vormgevingen van de Islam in Nederland gezien in Europees perspectief*, Werkdocumenten W118, The Hague: WRR.

Wetenschappelijke Raad voor het Regeringsbeleid (2001) *Towards a pan-European Union*, Reports to the Government no. 59, The Hague: Sdu Uitgevers.

Wetenschappelijke Raad voor het Regeringsbeleid (2002) *De toekomst van de nationale rechtsstaat*, Rapporten aan de Regering nr. 63, The Hague: Sdu Uitgevers.

Wetenschappelijke Raad voor het Regeringsbeleid (2003a) *Slagvaardigheid in de Europabrede Unie*, Rapporten aan de Regering nr. 65, The Hague: Sdu Uitgevers.

Wetenschappelijke Raad voor het Regeringsbeleid (2003b) *Waarden, normen en de last van het gedrag,* Amsterdam: Amsterdam University Press.

White, J.B. (2002) *Islamist mobilization in Turkey. A study in vernacular politics*, Seattle: University of Washington.

Yavuz, M.H. (2003) *Islamic Political Identity in Turkey*, Oxford: Oxford University Press.

Yesilkagit, K. (1997) 'Islamic Fundamentalism and the Role of the Turkish Military between 1980 and 1997', *Jason*, 5, 22, 8-13.

Zakaria, F. (1997) 'The Rise of Illiberal Democracy', *Foreign Affairs,* 76, 6, 22-43.

Zemni, S. (2002) 'Islam, European Identity and the Limits of Multiculturalism', 158-173 in: W.A. Shadid & P.S. van Koningsveld (eds.), *Religious Freedom and the Neutrality of the State: the Position of Islam and the European Union*, Leuven: Peeters.

Searching for the Fault-Line

A survey of the role of Turkish Islam in the accession of Turkey to the European Union in the light of the 'clash of civilisations'

Erik-Jan Zürcher and Heleen van der Linden

2004

CONTENTS

1   INTRODUCTION: TURKEY — FAULT-LINE, FRONTLINE OR TEST CASE?

Since the mid-1990s, the discussion on Turkey's potential accession to the European Union (EU) has not merely been conducted on the basis of criteria determining the state of democracy and human rights, security and the economy. The EU's dramatic eastward expansion has also prompted European writers and politicians in particular to reflect more generally on 'Europe's' fundamental characteristics and borders. It almost goes without saying that these discussions have become focused on the case of Turkey. After all, this is not merely the only country officially enjoying the prospect of full membership of the EEC/EC/EU for over forty years, but also the country that is perceived as being culturally least like the other member states.

In debates, the divergent cultural character of Turkey is generally linked to the fact that over 95 per cent of its population say that they are Muslims. Historically, a contributing factor to that perception is surely that for hundreds of years, Turkey, or rather, the Ottoman Empire, was the only Islamic superpower directly confronting Europe.

Those who voice objections to Turkey's inclusion into the EU on cultural or religious grounds, often base their arguments either explicitly or implicitly on American sociologist Samuel Huntington's theories on the so-called 'clash of civilisations'. Huntington first aired his ideas on the 'clash of civilisations' in the American journal, *Foreign Affairs* in 1993. What he said in his article, and what he further developed in 1996 in a book, is summarised below.

Since the birth of the system of international relations in the 16th and 17th centuries, roughly four phases can be distinguished in history. The first phase lasted until the French Revolution. International relations during this time were essentially conducted among sovereigns. The French Revolution changed this into a system of relations among nations. During both these phases, the international system was multipolar. In other words, there were many more or less equal players who together determined the course of war and peace. After the First World War, this system founded on nation-states came to an end. The rise of communism, and shortly thereafter of fascism and national socialism, marked the beginning of an international system built on competing ideological blocs. The conclusion of the Second World War did not end of this phase, but actually marked the beginning of the most ideological phase in the history of international relations. For fifty years, the Cold War froze the world to a bipolar system, in which the so-called Third World was the passive battlefield on which 'East' and 'West' fought out, or allowed others to fight out, their struggle for world domination.

In Huntington's view, the collapse of communism has created a fundamentally new situation. International relations are now no longer determined by two ideological blocs but by a multipolar system made up of nation-states. The policy orientation of these states – and this is the core idea of 'The Clash of Civilizations and the Remaking of World Order' – are now guided by cultural factors: solidarity within their own civilisation and antagonism towards other civilisations. Huntington perceives the world as divided into seven large cultural blocs (Chinese, Japanese, Hindu, Islamic, Orthodox, Western and Latin-American), and he expects the major conflicts of the future to be fought on the peripheries of these civilisations, in particular between 'the West', China, and 'Islam'. Civilisations as such will not be the actors within these large, worldwide conflicts, since they lack governments or armies. It is the dominant state within each civilisation, such as the United States, India or China, that will base its policies on its place within this 'civilisation'.

The 'clash of civilisations' has now become a household concept, and not just in the academic world. Huntington's thesis has been widely debated within political science and contemporary history, and reactions have mostly ranged from the critical to the outright dismissive. This applies both to the empirical foundation of his thesis (Huntington's factual knowledge is often dubious) and to the mentality it exudes, described by critics as 'intellectual tribalism'. He is often accused of unjustifiably suggesting that civilisations are monoliths rather than complex mosaics. In reality, George Bush's 'West' obviously differs from that of Woody Allen, and this is even more true for kaleidoscopic Europe.

Huntington's ideas have had an even larger impact outside academia, within politics and foreign policy. They emerge in all sorts of debates, often in dubious ways. Huntington unthinkingly adopted the Chinese nationalist notion that the fabulous rise of the Asian tiger economies was based on 'Confucian values'. Obviously, this was grist to the mills of authoritarian rulers such as Mahatir in Malaysia and Lee in Singapore, both of whom claimed that democracy and human rights were Western inventions that did not fit in with 'Asian values'.

In Huntington's view, the EU, too, is a cultural community whose eastward expansion has restored the traditional cultural border between western and eastern Christianity. (Thus, he conveniently bypasses the role of Greece.) In Europe, the ideas he expounded in his article of 1993 and his book of 1996 have influenced Christian-Democrats such as Kohl and Martens and liberals such as Bolkestein, prompting them to define Europe as a cultural community based on Christianity and humanism. From this they logically concluded that Islamic states such as candidate-member Turkey do not belong to Europe. In 2002, Chairman of the European Convention Giscard d'Estaing chose to repeat this standpoint.

In Huntington's worldview it is the Chinese and Islamic civilisations in particular which, from the strength of their own value systems, have evolved into rivals of Western liberal democracy. This view is clearly music to the ears of Islamic fundamentalists, who tend to see Islamic religion and culture as incompatible with 'Western' civilisation, including liberal democracy.

Is Islam the antithesis of Western civilisation? In that case, Turkey would seem to be the test case par excellence or, better still, the frontline where Huntington's theories can be tested. It is Europe's largest Muslim neighbour, a NATO member, an aspiring EU member, and a member of the Council of Europe and the OSCE. In addition, 95 per cent of its population consider themselves as Muslims, and it is the direct heir of the Ottoman Empire. For many centuries Ottoman sultans were Christian Europe's most important opponents. They ruled the Middle East and South-East Europe for four hundred years, representing the only Islamic sovereigns to claim the title of 'Defender of the Holy Sites' (Mecca and Medina).

89

In this survey we want to examine the validity of the widely held perception that there exists a cultural fault-line between Turkey and Europe, whose religious dimension makes its potential impact all the more destructive. In other words, does the fact that Turkey is an Islamic country, or rather that it has a predominantly Muslims population, also render it the odd man out who had better be excluded from the EU? Examining this question clearly also forces us to consider whether Huntington's thinking in terms of cultural blocs is meaningful and productive. Do the 'West' and 'Islam' really exist? And is the dividing line between those two 'blocs' really a frontline? Or does Turkey in fact enable us to see the contours of a symbiosis of Western and Islamic cultural elements?

To answer these questions, we have chosen the following approach. In the first part (chapter 2) we will begin by describing the most important aspects of contemporary Turkish Islam. The aim is to chart this in a way that reflects both the most significant properties of its Turkishness, and the multi-faceted nature of religious life in Turkey. Rather than conducting a general discussion on 'Islam', we examine it in its specific local and historical context. In other words, we describe the evolution and characteristics of Turkish Islam.

It should be emphasised, though, that in analysing a phenomenon such as 'Islam' or even 'Turkish Islam' we cannot possibly pretend to be exhaustive. Islam is both a doctrine or ideological system that tries to answer all the why's and wherefores of our existence, and a social phenomenon encompassing a wide range of actual manifestations.

In addition, it is not easy to indicate what should be considered as still a part of 'Islam' and what should not. Cultural codes, habits and traditions which in themselves have nothing to do with the doctrinal system of Islam, such as arranged marriages, honour killings and veiling, are often perceived by the outside world and especially the West, as typical of Islam. Traditional sections of the population uphold these customs, sanctify them and consider them as cornerstones of their faith. This report deals in particular with the position of Islam as a doctrinal system in Turkish society, even though ideology and cultural codes occasionally have some ground in common, such as in the case of the banning of headscarves from educational institutions. This is one of the frontlines of political conflict in Turkey.

In the first part, we have decided to cover the five most important aspects of Turkish Islam as a stepping stone for examining the extent to which Turkey has witnessed a symbiosis of EU values (such as democracy and human rights) and Islamic cultural heritage, or is likely to do so in future. The subjects under discussion are the relationship between Islam and the state; official doctrine versus Tarikats and neo-movements; Sunni Islam and Alevism; Islamic fundamentalism and the position of non-Muslims.

Based on these topics, we will return to our central question in the second part (chapter 3) dealing with sub-issues related to Turkey's ability to fit in with the EU. One example is the issue of Turkey's role in a common European cultural heritage, and another its compatibility with notions of democracy and human rights that have developed in Europe. And also: to what extent are the worldviews and lifestyles of Turks actually determined by their religion and what are the chances or risks of an Islamic fundamentalist victory? We will base the answers to these questions in part on the core texts of the different manifestations of Turkish Islam described in chapter 2. These involve texts as the pocket-catechism of so-called 'state-Islam', a publication by Necmettin Erbakan, the manifesto of the AK Party and a speech by a prominent modernist. We examine to what extent the statements in these texts contradict the core values ascribed to 'Western civilisation', and in this case to those of the EU. Based on these comparisons but for instance also on the results of surveys of the religious attitudes of the Turkish population, we try to provide more insight into Turkish receptiveness to Islamic fundamentalism. Working on the assumption that pluralism, such as in religion and the media, is a product of a democratic political system, we conclude the chapter by briefly considering the extent to which such pluralism is present in different areas. In the conclusion we subsequently return to Turkey's position within the framework of the 'clash of civilisations', and its implications for the country's EU accession.

2   TURKEY'S CURRENT ISLAMIC LANDSCAPE

This chapter describes the most important aspects of contemporary Turkish Islam. Since this contemporary landscape is the outcome of several radical transformations in the past, we will regularly refer back to crucial historical backgrounds that decisively shaped these important contemporary developments.

2.1   ISLAM AND THE STATE

2.1.1   THE '28 FEBRUARY PROCESS': CONFRONTATION BETWEEN RELIGION, SOCIETY AND STATE

On 28 June 1996, the Turkish Republic witnessed an event unprecedented in its history since its creation in 1923: a politician who explicitly allowed himself to be inspired, both politically and personally, by Islamic standards and values, was sworn in as prime minister. Necmettin Erbakan, the leader of the Welfare Party, owed this post to his election victory in December 1995 (when he received 21.3 per cent of the vote) and to the shrewd manner in which he had exploited the divisions among the other political parties. Erbakan's governing coalition, with the conservative, Western-oriented and secular True Path Party, seemed to herald a new era in modern Turkish history. However, it soon emerged that this development was anathema to the secular state machinery.

93

On 28 February 1997 the Turkish army leadership launched a campaign in which it identified 'Islamic fundamentalism' (*irtica*, literally: 'reactionary inclination) as the largest threat to Turkey's national security, worse than Kurdish separatism or foreign threats. Through the National Security Council, the very powerful body within which the military leadership advises the cabinet, the army presented a list of eighteen conditions that the Erbakan government had to fulfil. The implicit threat behind these demands was clear: the army would bring down the government if it failed to meet them. When the Erbakan government hesitated and dawdled with their fulfilment, the military organised a campaign in which the media, the judiciary, the bureaucracy and eventually also the parliamentary representatives of the True Path Party, were all lobbied and mobilised against the government. Trade unions and employers' organisation formed their own 'Secularist Front'. As a result of this pressure, the Erbakan government fell on 18 June 1997.

This '28 February process', which is denoted in Turkey as a 'soft' or 'postmodern' coup d'état', continued after the cabinet's fall. The measures that the military insisted on having implemented, were sweeping and far-reaching. One of their most important demands was the introduction of an eight-year period of primary education. Until then, primary schools in Turkey offered five years of education, after which many parents, either out of conviction or financial necessity, sent their children to Islamic schools for a further three-years of religious education. By setting compulsory state education at eight years, these so-called *imam-hatip okullar* (schools for pastoral care workers and preachers), lost their market. Many additional measures exacted by the military were also undertaken by Erbakan's successor in the years 1997 to 1999. In January 1998, the Constitutional Court ordered the dissolution of the Welfare Party and banned Erbakan from politics for a period of five years, a verdict later upheld by the European Court of Human Rights (Yavuz 2003: 3, 244).

The Constitutional Court's decision was based on articles 68 and 69 of the Turkish constitution, which had been introduced by an earlier military junta during its coup d'état in September 1980. These articles stated that no political party could be formed that "violates the principles of secular Republic" (art. 68), and that parties "exploiting religious sentiments, symbols or arguments" would be banned (art. 69). The Court's motivation was notable in that it emphasised that religion should not play a role in politics and social life, and that "religion controls the inner aspect of the individual, while secularism controls the outward aspect of the individual." The court thus strictly followed in the footsteps of Kemalism, the Turkish state ideology taking shape since the 1920s (Yavuz 2003: 247).

For a better understanding of the positions and arguments of the main players in this confrontation between religion, society and state, we will examine two factors that shaped the current situation. The first concerns ideas on state and religion during the Ottoman Empire (1300-1922), the direct predecessor of the Republic of Turkey; the second concerns the process of secularisation, which began around 1840 under the Ottoman Empire and in the Turkish Republic reached its zenith between 1923 and 1945.

2.1.2 ISLAM AND THE STATE UNDER THE OTTOMANS

The Ottoman-Islamic heritage of the Republic of Turkey, in turn, represents a tradition that draws from two very divergent and partly conflicting sources: firstly, the Islamic roots of society and, secondly, the Turkish tradition of state formation and state constitution which had taken shape in Central Asia by the 6th century and in the Middle East by the 10th century.

The oldest Islamic community, which sprung up around the prophet Mohammed in 622 in Yathrib, later Medina, was an autonomous community. Its leaders derived their legitimacy from religious charisma and they governed muslims in war and in peace. Logically, the rules creating the foundation of this early Islamic community did not anticipate a state above or beyond the community of believers. The lives of the faithful were governed by a system of religious standards and rules, supervised by religious leaders. In the beginning, these were Mohammed and his direct successors (the 'rightful caliphs') but leadership soon became the pre-eminent field for religious specialists, the Islamic scholars (the ulema). The ulema expanded the pronunciations in the Koran and the traditions of the workings and teachings of the prophet Mohammed into a system of laws (the sharia, or şeriat in Turkish). This formed the basis for communal and personal life. In the eyes of the Muslims, the şeriat was and is God's work. Its rules can be interpreted, but in principle it is immutable; legislation by humans is impossible.

In the 9th century, two hundred years after the actions of Mohammed, Islam assumed a more orthodox character when the free interpretation of the şeriat by individual legal scholars ceased to be considered legitimate. Since that time, interpretation had to be restricted to debates on the works of earlier exegetists, whose work therefore assumed enormous authority (Yerasimos et al. 2000: 13-15; Mardin 1989: 20-21).

The rapid conquest of regions ranging from Spain in the west to India in the east inevitably led to the creation of a solid governance system, i.e. a state. The attitude of Islamic legal scholars towards the state was ambivalent from the start. On the one hand, the state was an essential institution for maintaining religious order and fulfilling God's plan for humanity. Without protection by the state, the true faith could not survive in an evil world. On the other hand, there was a widespread notion that power corrupts and that state governance could not go hand in hand with a pious and good life (Lewis 1996: 157-8). That this was seen as an inevitability can be illustrated with an Ottoman example: not one of the Ottoman sultans between 1300 and 1922 ever undertook the *hadj*, the pilgrimage to Mecca that is, in principle, compulsory for every Muslim. Religious scholars all agreed that the political duty of the sultan to protect the 'house of islam' (*dar-ul-islam*), ranked above his personal salvation.

In the eyes of the ulema, the ideal Islamic state was a theocracy that had God as the exclusive source of legitimacy and justice. At the same time, Muslims realised that in order to keep government institutions operational, their worldly ruler and 'God's shadow on earth' had to formulate rules and impose punishments to supplement the body of rules already anchored into religious law. This authority of sovereigns was denoted in Arabic as *siyâsa* (living on in modern Turkish as 'politics': *siyaset*) or its equivalents, such as *urf* (Turkish: *örf*). To proclaim these kind of rules and regulations, sovereigns required authorisation by leading religious experts, who had to certify that the rules were indeed supplementary, and not contradictory to the şeriat (Lewis 1996: 223-4).

From the 10th century on, almost the entire core region of Islam came under the rule of Turkish dynasties originating from the Central Asian steppes. Virtually all of these dynasties had converted to Islam in Central Asia, prior to their invasion of the Middle East. In addition, they also brought with them the strong military and political traditions developed by the Turks. In the border regions between the Middle East and Central Asia, these traditions blended with the ancient Persian monarchical tradition, that strongly emphasised the independent authority of the sovereign.

Partly inspired by the Persian kingdoms they encountered en route, the Turkish dynasties embraced the Sunni type of Islam and, more specifically, the Hanifite school of religious thought. This has influenced the way in which subsequent Turkish dynasties have shaped the relationship between state and Islam. Of the four schools of religious thought within Sunni Islam, the Hanifite school offers the greatest opportunity for 'Realpolitik'. Hanafite theory on rule simply defines the legitimate ruler as he who manages to come to power and hold on to it (Imber 1997: 24, 67). For the Turkish newcomers from the steppes, whose power depended on the sword, this was obviously quite attractive. As their power increased, however, they also developed additional arguments supporting the legitimacy of their authority. These included invented genealogies and, in the case of the Ottomans, the myth of the 'transfer' of the caliphate to the Ottoman sultan by the last Arab Abbasid caliph.

More than any other dynasty, the Ottomans succeeded in uniting Islamic and Turkish-Persian traditions into a single administrative system. Formally, the Ottoman Empire was an Islamic state, whose ruler, the sultan, had to protect the land of the Muslims and ensure their opportunities to live as good Muslims within its borders. Also formally, divine law or şeriat formed the foundation of the legal system. In practice, the şeriat's effectiveness was largely limited to what we would call the realm of private law: family law and contract law. Everything that we today would consider as public law, in particular all aspects of public order and public administration, was regulated in collections of edicts (*kanun*, from the Byzantine canon) published in the name of the sultan. Obviously, these two legal systems were in force in different regions. The şeriat was the law of the Islamic community, both inside and outside the Empire; Muslims in

South-East Asia or China also organised their personal lives according to this law. Yet the şeriat was not applicable to the largely autonomous Christian and Jewish communities inside the Empire. As the law of the state, however, the kanun applied to all subjects inside the state's borders.

It was the task of the leading ulema, in particular of the highest-ranking mufti (legal adviser) of the Empire, the *şeyhülislam*, to harmonise the sacred law and the edicts of the sultan (Poulton 1997: 34-5). This implied that the religious authorities and the palace were caught in a mutual embrace. Since the sultan pretended to be not just an Islamic sovereign but *the* Islamic sovereign par excellence, he could ill-afford losing the legitimacy provided by Islamic legal scholars. This being said, the Ottoman sultans were much more successful than their predecessors in incorporating the ulema into the state apparatus by a system of strict appointments and controls. This clearly provided the court with a whole repertory of levers on an uncooperative ulema.

Thus, despite the theocratic ideal of Islamic legal scholarship, the Ottoman state was de facto a secular administrative apparatus whose policies were legitimised by religion. As the 'great tradition' with a hegemonic nature, Islam acted as the cultural and political bridge between the state elite and the masses, who were predominantly Sunni Muslims (Yavuz 2003: 38-9). Without this kind of sacralising, it is unlikely that the Ottoman Empire could have retained the loyalty of its Islamic population and survived for six hundred years.

97

2.1.3   SECULARISATION IN THE OTTOMAN EMPIRE

From the facts above we can also conclude that the oft-heard cliché that Islam has never known the separation of 'church and state' represents a huge distortion of reality. Its origins from an autonomous community meant that in Islam, or at least among its legal scholars, theory formation on the state is rather poor. By contrast, Turkish Islamic states, in particular the Ottoman Empire, developed an extensive and codified practice of de facto secular governance. Political legitimacy was in essence two-fold: Islam and state (or sovereign) were both sources of legislation (Mardin 1989: 21). It was this highly practical dual system of religiously sanctioned rules and institutions which essentially stemmed from the autonomous authority of the sovereign, that in the 19th century would start off processes of modernisation and secularisation.

In the latter part of the 18th century and the beginning of the 19th century, the Ottoman Empire suffered several traumatic defeats at the hands of European states. In 1774, 1792 and 1829 wars were lost to Russia. There are two reasons why this had catastrophic consequences for the authority of the Ottoman sultan. Firstly, the Ottomans lost control of the Black Sea, on which they were dependent for food supplies to their capital Istanbul. Secondly, the sultan had to cede areas inhabited by Muslim populations to non-Islamic rulers (the Russian tsar). In the same period, the then Ottoman province of Egypt was occupied by Napoleon Bonaparte (1798-1801). As a result, European rulers, for the first time since the crusades, obtained one of the heartlands of the Islamic Middle East, including the Empire's second city, Cairo.

The shock of these defeats prompted a group of reform-minded administrators in Istanbul to call for the modernisation of Ottoman state institutions on European models. The prime example for this modernisation was France, both the France of the Bourbon dynasty and that of the Revolution and Napoleon. After being ousted from power in 1808, these reformers were able to pursue their policies again after 1826, under the autocratic reign of Sultan Mahmut II (r. 1808-1839). Initially, their reforms aimed at strengthening both the internal and external powers of the central state. Their first concern was the modernisation of the army, but once a European-style army was formed, their reform efforts spread unchecked. Factories were needed for uniforms, training institutes for officers, population registers to facilitate conscription and efficient tax-collection systems to pay for it all.

Throughout the 19th century, the Ottoman Empire slowly took on the appearance of a typically modern state. There were state schools in every town, postal services, railways, clock towers (with a unified time for the whole Empire) and lighthouses, museums, population censuses, birth certificates and passports. The small state apparatus of the beginning of the 19th century grew sixty-fold and assumed the typical characteristics of a bureaucracy.

The 1839 edict announcing the sultan's intention to implement wide-ranging reforms (the 'Hatti Şerif of Gülhane' or 'Noble Edict of the Rose Chamber'), explicitly paid lip service to religious law. Its preamble stated that "countries not governed by şeriat could not continue to exist" (Deringil 1998: 9). Yet the measures themselves had little if anything to do with religious law. They actually had secularising side effects, be it initially only implicitly. Pupils training for doctors and veterinarians at the new schools, and the engineers and artillery officers dealing with modern mathematics, for instance, all became the bearers of a materialistic, scientific worldview.

During the 1850s and 1860s, secularisation also acquired a legal and institutional face through the introduction of new, European-inspired, law books such as the criminal code or the commercial code and the institution of new courts, councils and ministries based on the European model. The şeriat was never rendered inoperative, but its area of implementation kept shrinking. Since the new procedures and laws were largely based on the French model, they also reflected legal practice in this fortress of *laïcité* (Dumont in Landau (ed.) 1984: 35-37).

As in other European monarchies, the purely traditional concept of a God-given monarchy legitimised solely by religion and tradition, also became increasingly a subject for discussion in the Ottoman Empire after 1848. Pushed by rising nationalism among the non-Islamic population groups and, from 1860 onwards also, by a fledgling liberal movement, there began a quest for a new type of legitimacy with national and democratic dimensions (Hobsbawm 1990: 84). The Ottoman Empire's power elite concluded that having obedient subjects at the state's disposal no longer sufficed. Rivalry with European states meant that the state should be able to appeal to the masses to mobilise national forces. The Empire's subjects thus had to be moulded into Ottoman citizens who identified with 'their' state. If this were ever possible, it could only be done by granting them a say in the state's governance through a process of implicit negotiations (Deringil 1998: 45). Since the Ottoman Empire was, until 1878, still a state of which forty per cent of all citizens were non-Muslims, this therefore also implied a process of secularisation.

During the approximately twenty-year period between 1856 and 1876, this 'ottomanism' (Turkish term: *ittihadi anasır*, unity of the elements) provided an ideological guideline for political activity. It eventually culminated in the proclamation of the Ottoman constitution and in elections for the first Ottoman parliament, both in 1876. The constitution made no mention of a state religion and non-Muslims were proportionally represented in parliament. At the same time, however, constitution and parliament were still advocated with reference to Islamic arguments, as had been the case with the first great reformation decree less than forty years earlier. This line of argumentation was embedded in a discourse shaped during the 1860 by a group of young bureaucrats, the so-called 'Young Ottomans'. They defended liberal values using Islamic arguments and tried to show, through reinterpretation of Koranic texts and Islamic traditions, that democracy was actually intrinsic to Islam (Zürcher 1995: 80; Mardin 1979: 381-443).

In this respect, the lost war of 1877-1888 against Russia represented a watershed. It had followed a dramatic course and had ended with Russian troops entering the suburbs of Istanbul. The Ottoman Empire's subsequent loss of territory under the Treaty of Berlin prompted large groups of

Muslims to leave the Balkan and Caucus regions, thus radically changing the Empire's population make-up. After 1878, more than eighty per cent were Muslims. Ottoman citizenship, as laid down in the constitution and in parliament, had not been able to protect the country from disaster. Its ideological foundations had thus been discredited, and the state now faced the task of finding another ideological vehicle to unite the shaken Empire's newcomers and native populations (Yavuz 2003: 43-44).

During the long reign of Sultan Abdülhamit II (r. 1876-1909) the goalposts were moved. This Ottoman sultan, who now also strongly emphasised his religious function as caliph, launched an ideological offensive aimed at creating a new foundation for solidarity among the Empire's Muslim subjects. Like the Hapsburgs in the Austro-Hungarian Empire and the Romanov's Russia, the Ottomans answered the threats of nationalism and liberalism by launching an 'official nationalism' whose strong religious undertones should provide the monarchy with a new mysticism and power of expression (Deringil 1998: 47, 67; Anderson 1991: 83-111).

The Ottoman court's ambitions to employ Islam as social cement and a means for bolstering state-power, prompted unprecedented state interference both with the content and the spread of the faith. Islam had to be loyal to the state, uniform and controllable on a scale hitherto unknown. Thus, there emerged regulations for publishers of the Koran, for religious education at schools and for sermons in the mosques. The most important outcome of this standardising of Islam by the state was the codification, modelled on a European code, of religious law, the Mecelle. This standard text, the fruit of many years' work by a state commission, was distributed to the far-flung corners of the Empire (Deringil 1998: 50).

Sultan Abdülhamit's Islam policy was in no way a simple reversion to old Ottoman traditions. Its ideological drive paralleled an enormous expansion of modern education, means of communications (telegraph-lines, railways) and printing. The modern state, with its aspirations to regulate the lives of its citizens right down to the finest detail, was born in this era, and the Republic of Turkey would be inconceivable without the legacy of Abdülhamit.

The constitutional revolution of July 1908 led directly to the reinstatement of the constitution and of parliament, which had been suspended in 1878. Indirectly (in April 1909) it also caused the fall of Sultan Abdülhamit. Both these events were the doing of the so-called 'Young Turks', young officers and civil servants who had been schooled in the modern, European-inspired educational institutions that had been developed under the reign of Abdülhamit. These Young Turks saw the old regime as corrupt and powerless, particularly against Europe, and they considered the time ripe for a national revival. In their view, a constitutional parliamentary regime provided not a goals in itself but merely one of several technical devices to bring about this revival (Hanioğlu 1995: 214-16).

The regime of the Young Turks, which would last from 1908 until 1918, was in some respects a continuation of Abdülhamit's regime. These Young Turks, who almost all came from the ranks of state civil servants, also strived for an increase in state power and for centralisation and standardization. This quickly brought them into conflict with the non-Islamic population of the Empire, who had expected the constitutional revolution to provide exactly the opposite, i.e. decentralisation and even autonomy. After the start of the Balkan War (1912), when the Ottoman Empire was attacked by four Christian Balkan states, the 'Muslim/non-Muslim' antithesis had become the fault-line running through the entire society (see also sect. 2.5). As in the time of Abdülhamit, the Young Turks mobilised the population on the basis of a nationalist ideology whose unifying element was Islam, or at least belonging to an Islamic population group (Zürcher: Karpat (ed.) 2000: 150-179).

101

Paradoxically, the Young Turks, who propagated a nationalism based on religious 'markers', were anything but devoted or traditional Muslims. They were heavily influenced by materialism and positivism. They saw the role of Islam primarily as that of social cement, and were simultaneously driven by a strong anticlericalism. Islam had to be cleared from its superstitious mysticism and from the narrow conservatism of its ulema. Such elements should no longer be allowed to influence the administration, nor hinder the freedom of thought (Zürcher, 'Ottoman sources of Kemalist thought'). The resulting 'true' Islam would be progressive and open to science and technology. According to some of the more extreme Young Turkish writers, Islam was not only the pre-eminently rational religion, but it was actually identical to positivism. Islam needed to be made consistent with science, or as Abdullah Cevdet, one of the most secularist of the Young Turkish thinkers, put it: "Religion is the science of the masses and science is the religion of the elite" (Hanioğlu 1997: 133-158).

Several conceptions of the Young Turks did indeed lead to concrete measures that limited the authority of the religious experts and the holy law still further and that also increased the state's grip on Islam. In 1916, the şeyhülislam, the highest mufti, lost his cabinet seat and his ministry was downgraded to a department. He lost his jurisdiction over the religious courts to the Ministry of Justice, while the administration of religiously inspired foundations, the *evkaf*, was transferred to the Ministry of Finance. The latter measure was very drastic indeed, since all religious and charitable institutes in the Empire, such as mosques, *medreses* (religious academies), hospitals and libraries, depended financially on foundations which had been set up by benefactors in an earlier age. Islamic institutions thus lost their financial independence and religious schools were now placed under the supervision of the Ministry of Education. In 1917, the government also had the family law re-codified. While it is true that the customs of the different religious communities (for Muslims, the rules of the şeriat) remained intact, the mere fact that the state judiciary could now supervise the implementation of these rules, was a step in the direction of secularism. The adoption in 1917 of the European (Gregorian) calendar further highlighted the separation of state and Islam (Dumont in Landau (ed.) 1984: 37-38).

In terms of both their underlying world view and actual measures, the Young Turks during this period paved the way for the future 'Kemalist revolution' that would take shape in the Republic of Turkey in the 1920s.

2.1.4 THE KEMALIST IDEAL

Unlike for the rest of Europe, for Turkey (and in a way also for Russia) the First World War ended in 1922 rather than 1918. Through a bitter war of independence, fought not directly against the victors of the First World War, Great Britain and France, but against their local allies, the Armenians in the east and the Greeks in the west, the Ottomans managed to reverse a further subdivision of what remained of their Empire. This victory eventually materialised in the Treaty of Lausanne (1923), through which present-day Turkey appeared on the map as an independent national state. As a result of this victory, there was no longer a need to appeal to religion for mobilising the population. From 1923, all attention could thus be devoted to developing the country.

Mustafa Kemal Pasja (after 1934: Atatürk), the leader of the independence struggle and after October 1923 the first president of the new Republic of Turkey, belonged to a radical faction of the Young Turks. They shared a deep conviction that only rationalism and knowledge could serve as the basis upon which to accelerate Turkey's modernisation. Their discourse on Islam perfectly matched that of the Young Turks prior to 1918. Time and again, Mustafa Kemal emphasised he was not against Islam, because 'true' Islam was a rational and natural religion. At the same time, he seized every possible opportunity to attack the ulema and in particular those religious leaders that were not linked to the state, such as Sufi sheikhs, miracle workers and holy men. Islam, as propagated by Kemal, was a personal conviction which required no intermediaries between God and the individual.

In practice, these views resulted in various confrontations with Islamism in Turkey. Firstly, the process was completed of bringing religious institutions wholly under state control. The state itself became officially secular in 1928. Secondly, in 1924 the caliphate was abolished, as was separate religious education. True, the 1924 constitution did record Islam as the state religion, but this passage was deleted in 1928. The function of şeyhülislam was abolished, and replaced by a new body, the Directorate of Religious Affairs (*Diyanet İşleri Başkanlığı, Diyanet*), which fell directly under the premier. This body had complete authority over all religious aspects of Turkish life, controlling mosques, sacred tombs and Dervish monasteries (until they were closed in 1925), and appointing not only preachers (imams) and other functionaries connected to the mosques, but also all muftis (advisors on matters of faith). From its new capital in Ankara, it supplied instructions on the content of both sermons and religious advice. Paradoxically, the secular Republic of Turkey thus appropriated greater religious authority than the sultan-caliph ever had (Dumont in Landau (ed.) 1984: 38).

These measures were in fact the epilogue to a century of secularisation of institutions, providing a logical continuation of the measures taken by the Young Turks in 1916-1917. The position of the ulema was even further undermined when in 1926 the sacred law was abolished in family law, which had been its only remaining area of enforcement. The substitution of the 19th-century codification of the şeriat, the *Mecelle*, for an adaptation of the Swiss civil code, was a radical step that is still unique in the present-day Islamic world.

103

Whereas state-linked Islamism was brought under strict control, autonomous Islamic movements, especially the mystical brotherhoods (*tarikats*), were simply abolished in 1925. Dervish monasteries (*tekkes*), which formed the local centres of the brotherhoods, were closed, as were the sacred tombs (*türbes*), which were often popular places of pilgrimage. The issue of the tarikats, their role in the society and their legacy is of such importance that it is dealt with separately in section 2.2.

Measures such as the introduction of Swiss family law or the banning of dervish orders had a direct impact on the personal lives of people from all walks of life, thus causing considerably more dissatisfaction and protest than the earlier abolition of institutions such as the caliphate or the function of şeyhülislam. The same was true for several other measures which can probably best be described as outright attacks on Islamic culture. The 1920s and 1930s were a period in which Turkey's outward appearance changed dramatically as a result of legislation that overhauled the public experience of space and time. Dress codes banning traditional headdress, the introduction of the European calendar and European clocks, the replacement of Arabic writing with the Latin alphabet, the laying-out of parks and terraces, the erection of statues of Atatürk – all these were actions not directly relating to faith, but clearly involving a reorientation away from Middle Eastern culture and towards Europe. However, in many cases the masses took this message as an attack on religion. In the Middle East, head-dress had for centuries served as a distinguishing element to identify a person's social and religious standing, while Arabic writing was immediately associated with the language of the Koran, especially by villagers whose only contact with written culture was mosque-related. Thus the cultural offensive had strong anti-Islamic connotations (Zürcher 1993: 194-197).

The metamorphosis of at least the urban part of Turkey also deeply impressed foreigners. Countless visitors stated their admiration for the 'new' Turkey in books with such revealing titles as *The Veils have Dropped!* or *Allah Dethroned.* These writers generally had no idea of what had happened in the one hundred years preceding the secularisation of Turkey, ascribing these changes exclusively to Atatürk's Republic.

During the first twenty years of its existence, top-ranking highly-educated Ottoman ulema could provide the Republic with religious knowledge. Unlike their Young Turkish predecessors, who had tried to modernise the curricula of religious training colleges, the Kemalists thought little of reforming training colleges for the ulema. Thus, in 1930-1931 the county's two-dozen colleges for imams and preachers were closed and in 1935, its only remaining theological faculty, at the University of Istanbul, underwent the same fate. The long-term effect was to create a lost generation, a 'missing link' in Turkish Islam and a breach in the great Ottoman tradition of religious scholarship.

The fact that the Kemalists actually pursued a policy of driving back Islam from public life, reflected their awareness of their own minority position. They saw themselves as the teachers of a backward nation, whose mission it was to drag the people, kicking and screaming, into the modern world according to the Kemalist maxim, 'despite the people for the people' (*halka rağmen halk için*). They recognised the mobilising power of Islamic slogans and were constantly on the look-out for 'religious reaction' (*irtica*). This term, which is still today continuously used by secularists in Turkey, first became fashionable during the Islam-inspired counterrevolution of April 1909, which had been a traumatic event for the entire generation of Young Turks to which Atatürk and his followers also belonged. Less than a year after the constitutional revolution, the 'liberators' were driven from the capital by a mob chanting Islamic slogans. Even though troops led by Young Turks managed to end the revolt within two weeks, the mortal danger of a politically exploited Islam was indelibly printed in the memory of the Young Turks. Under the Republic, they continued to interpret any signs of opposition in this light. This was true of the Kurdish uprising in 1925, the murder in 1930 of a reserve officer by a group of Dervish in Menemen near Izmir, the rise of Sait Nursî and many more minor incidents (see also sect. 2.2.6). Fear of a combination of malevolent Islamic reactionaries and underdeveloped, manipulable popular masses, has motivated hardline Kemalists to this day.

This tough anti-Islamic policy stance was continued by Atatürk's successors after his death in 1938 until, for a variety of reasons, the ending of the Second World War made it impossible to pursue.

2.1.5   TWO INTERPRETATIONS OF SECULARISM

Almost immediately after the end of the Second World War in Europe, İsmet İnönü, Atatürk's successor as president and leader of the party, signalled that Turkey would embark on the road to democracy. There were both external and domestic reasons for choosing this path. Turkey had remained neutral for practically the entire war, but at the very end had joined the United Nations (UN) and had also signed its charter. From 1946 on, it emerged that Turkey was being subjected to intense pressure from the Soviet Union, which it could not withstand without assistance. With the declaration of the Truman Doctrine in 1947 and the availability of Marshall Aid, the United States became Turkey's most important political and economic partner, and fulfilling American demands in the spheres of democratisation and economic liberalism became a matter of life and death. At the same time, domestic tension had increased considerably throughout the war years, which for most people had been years of authoritarian oppression and impoverishment.

In 1946, Turkey became a multi-party democracy. This immediately affected the relationship between the state and Islam. Competition for electoral support now really began to matter, and over 75 per cent of the voters still lived in rural areas. Both there and in the small provincial towns, a conservative, strongly religious outlook dominated which had hardly been touched by the Kemalist cultural revolution. In its quest for electoral support, the government allowed Islam some more breathing space. Islamic education at school, albeit optional for the moment, was reintroduced and the theological faculty was reopened. A few training programmes for preachers re-appeared, and in 1948, for the first time in a generation, some Turks could make the pilgrimage to Mecca. The final cabinet of the Kemalist regime (1949-1950) was even led by Şmsettin Günaltay, a professor of Islamic theology.

It was all to no avail. Despite its u-turn, the Republican People's Party which had upheld 25 years of authoritarian and secularist policy, had lost all credibility in the eyes of the population. The May 1950 elections were won, with a large majority, by the opposition Democratic Party under the leadership of Adnan Menderes. In contrast to the Republican People's Party, the Democratic Party had derived its power from the backing of local networks, which in the 1950s discovered the value of their support. This made the party sensitive to the needs and perceptions of the people. As a result, the Democratic Party and its successors have often been accused by secularists in Turkey of exploiting religious policies and gambling with Atatürk's legacy. But this is at most a half-truth.

It is true that Menderes made concessions to the religious sentiments of the population. One of the first things he did was allowing the *azan* (call to prayer) to be made in Arabic again. Furthermore, religious education in schools was expanded and more training programmes for imams and preachers sprung up. The sale of religious literature was permitted and the Democratic Party sought the support of religious movements such as the Nurcus (sect. 2.2.6) during elections. Even so, there was no meddling whatsoever with the secular character of the state and legislation. A return to Islamic legislation or a relaxation of state control over muftis and mosques was never considered. When in 1950 a group of radical religious activists of the Ticani Dervish order vandalised busts of Atatürk, a strict law preventing the desecration of Atatürk's memory was immediately pushed through parliament (Zürcher 1993: 243-5; Yavuz 2003: 61-2). Menderes and his followers reacted outspokenly to the continuous accusations by the Republican People's Party that they were undermining secularism. Against the Kemalist view of secularism as a defence mechanism protecting the freedom of thought from Islamic interference, they proposed a secularism that would guarantee citizen's freedom of religion. Secularism should not be anti-religious and should be limited to matters of state and constitution.

Although the Turkish army repeatedly intervened in the political process, notably through the coup of May 1960 and the 'coup by memorandum' of March 1971, and also through several warnings and demonstrations in the intermediate period, the political current represented by Menderes remained the dominant political force throughout the 1960s and 1970s. After 1965, the successor to the Democratic Party, Süleyman Demirel's True Path Party, managed to attract the majority of the Democratic Party's former supporters. The Islam policy of this large conservative people's party remained largely identical to that of Menderes' party. Demirel stated repeatedly that, although the state was secular and should remain so, this did not mean that the individual should also be secular. Islam was appreci-

ated as a moral code that provided strength to Turkish society. During the
Cold War years, politicians of a more conservative orientation even saw
Islamic standards and values, along with Kemalist nationalism, as an essential counterweight to the threats of socialism and communism. Religious
movements benefited from this view by becoming even more integrated
into the mainstream of Turkish politics (Yavuz 2003: 62).

2.1.6   ISLAM IN POLITICS AND 'STATE-ISLAM'

Apart from a growing interest in Islam by non-religious parties, the 1960s
also witnessed the rise of explicitly Islamic, or Islamist, political movements. That is to say, movements whose political manifesto are (also)
based on Islamic guidelines. The new constitution that was adopted in
1961, gave more room to Islamic political movements.

The rise of an Islamic political movement was not due to an increase in
piety among the population, but to the specific socio-economic developments of the 1960s. These were the years when Turkey built up a large and
powerful industrial sector and also saw the rise of a considerable, and
frequently militant, labour movement. The *esnaf* (small entrepreneurs)
had increasing difficulties identifying with the policies of the larger parties,
which were strongly geared to big business (in the case of the Justice Party)
or to civil servants and organised labour (the Republican People's Party).
By the end of the 1960s, these small entrepreneurs had managed to take
over the control of the Union of Chambers of Commerce of Turkey from
the big industrialists in Istanbul. Their representative became the president. This was Necmettin Erbakan, a partially German-educated professor
of mechanical engineering at the Technical University of Istanbul, who in
1969 was elected to parliament as an independent representative for the
conservative town of Konya. In 1970, together with a few other parliamentarians, he formed the National Order Party, which was banned for anti-
secular activities when in March 1971 the Turkish army seized power
behind the scenes. In 1973, Erbakan became the leader of a new party, or
rather, his old party under a new name: the National Salvation Party. It
gave a leading role to members of religious brotherhoods, in particular to
members of a branch of the Nakşibendis (sect. 2.2.4). Erbakan also
belonged, and still belongs, to this order.

Since 1973, the ideology of Erbakan's party was referred to as 'National
Vision' (Milli Görüş). Its manifesto included typically Islamist points, such
as an emphasis on ethics and morality in education and upbringing, as well
as the fight against usury and corruption. Surprisingly, though, the manifesto also strongly emphasised secularism. Freedom of opinion and freedom
of expression were qualified as the foundations of democracy and human

107

rights. However, it was a different interpretation of secularism than that of the Kemalists. What was meant was complete freedom of religion, without state control. The Kemalist notion of secularism was rejected as the 'dictatorship of the non-believers'. From the start, therefore, Erbakan's political agenda gave priority to the withdrawal of all articles from the penal code and the constitution that banned the political uses of religion (Erbakan 1975).

In the changeable climate of the 1970s, with increasing labour unrest and political and societal dislocation resulting from the economic crisis, the National Salvation Party proved attractive to a sizeable part of the traditionally-oriented electorate. In the 1973 elections, it received twelve per cent of the vote, thus becoming essential in helping coalitions gain a majority. It subsequently used this power to fill all strategic posts in 'its' ministries with its own party members.

In the eyes of the voters, the party's participation in established politics meant that it also shared responsibility for the policies that had failed to end the economic crisis and to quell political violence in the streets. In the 1977 elections, therefore, support for the party dropped to under nine per cent. However, National Salvation Party activists remained firmly in control of parts of the state apparatus. When the military intervened in September 1980, Erbakan's party was banned, along with all other political organisations. Erbakan himself was prosecuted, though finally acquitted. In the 1980s, the core of the party's activities shifted to Europe, where supporters of National Vision had much more room to manoeuvre than in Turkey itself (Zürcher in Driessen (ed.) 1997: 365-7).

The other islamist political movement that acquired influence in the 1970s and 1980s was the so-called 'Turkish-Islamist Synthesis'. This ideology was systematically developed in the 1970s by the writer İbrahim Kafesoğlu. It assumed that Islam had a special appeal to Turks, since the original Islam of the prophet Mohammed had a lot in common with the culture of the Central Asian Turks. They shared a high regard for justice, monotheism, a belief in the immortal soul and a strong devotion to family and decency. Therefore, it was the Turkish people's mission to be exceptional 'soldiers of Islam'. For the supporters of this ideology, Islam and the National Vision were inextricably linked to modern Turkish culture.

The Turkish-Islamist Synthesis was first embraced by an organisation calling itself the 'Hearth-fires of the Enlightened Souls' (*Aydın Ocakları*). It was a club set up in 1970 by leading figures from business, politics and university which aimed at challenging all the left-wing intellectuals who used to control political and ideological discussion in those days. They would be taken on with their own weapons: conferences, forums, publications, etc. Despite the secular Kemalist tradition of the Turkish officer's corps, quite a few members of the military were interested in this movement. In the second half of the 1970s, the Synthesis ideology also gained popularity amongst supporters of the Nationalist Action Party. Created from yet another splinter party in 1969, this was a radical (reactionary) right-wing party led be an ex-colonel, Alpsalan Türkes. Its support came mainly from conservative Sunni Turks residing in the wide belt bisecting Anatolia, where the population is heavily mixed (Turks vs Kurds and Sunnis vs Alevis). During the early years of its existence, it propagated an ultra-nationalistic brand of Kemalism, but by the mid-1970s the Turkish-Islamist Synthesis obtained the upper hand.

Türkes's Nationalist Action Party was even more successful than Erbakan's National Salvation Party in acquiring support from the poorly educated and impoverished youth of the city slums. These places were the breeding grounds for the young stormtrooper-like commandoes who, under the banner of 'Idealists' (*Ülkücü*), and wearing their Grey Wolf emblem, captured the streets from left-wing activists. Türkes's party was also banned after the 1980 coup d'état and, like Erbakan, he was prosecuted but eventually acquitted (Zürcher in Driessen (ed.) 1997: 367).

109

In 1980, a junta led by General Kenan Evren, the son of an imam, took control. He did not stop at banning the other religiously-oriented parties, but instead unleashed an all-inclusive ideological offensive, in which Islam occupied a central role. The Islam that was officially approved and propagated by the military leadership, had much in common with the Turkish-Islamist Synthesis. A few leading members of the 'Hearth-fires of the Enlightened Souls' also played major roles in shaping this new ideology (Yavuz 2003, 71-73). It had a strong nationalist character, emphasised the link between state and nation, national unity and social harmony and it glorified military and authoritarian values. In addition, Islam was presented as an 'enlightened' religion, open to science and technology (Evren 1986: 221). The goal of this ideological offensive was to render Turkish youth immune to both socialist propaganda and the temptations of radical Islamic movements that were not controlled by the state.

The islamisation of state ideology also dictated a radical reinterpretation of the legacy of Mustafa Kemal Atatürk. He was now presented as a reformer of Islam. And secularism was presented as a necessary step in purifying Islam and creating a 'true Islam' (Yavuz 2003: 70-1).

Starting in 1982, this 'state-Islam' was mostly propagated through education. It formed the basis of the National Cultural Report (1983) of the State Planning Bureau (Poulton 1997: 184). Lessons in religion and ethics were made compulsory for all classes and the state-controlled media (radio and television) also spread the message. The Directorate of Religious Affairs remained just as tied to the state as before, but in 1982 its existence and tasks were constitutionally fixed. These tasks reflected the close ties between religion and nationalism that were now propagated. The Directorate had to "protect the Turkish national identity" – a phrase borrowed directly from Kafesoğlu's original programme (Poulton 1997: 185-7). Materially, it profited from this new policy line: staff membership grew from 50,765 in 1979 to 84,172 ten years later. That the spread of 'correct' Islam was not limited to Turkey, could be witnessed by the Directorate's staff numbers working in Europe, which increased from 20 to 628 over the same period (Poulton 1997: 185-7).

Curiously, when observing this instrumentalisation of Islam as the state's ideological weapon by the military and its successors in the 1980s, one is somehow strongly reminded of the policies of Sultan Abdülhamit II, exactly a century earlier.

2.1.7 ISLAMIC BREAKTHROUGH AND KEMALIST REVIVAL

The Islam policy of the military rulers is often described as paving the way for the Islamist breakthrough during the 1994 and 1995 elections of Erbakan's re-created and renamed Welfare Party (of 1983) (Sunier 1998: 23-4). The idea behind this is that, once you open the door to Islam, there is no longer a choice of what kind of Islam may enter. Demographic developments, however, certainly also played role. The 1980s and early 1990s witnessed a period of unprecedented migration into Turkey's main cities. A city like Istanbul doubled in size in this period, and its new migrants formed the majority of the urban (municipal) electorate. In this new environment, the existence of migrants depended heavily on private networks and mystical brotherhoods (sect. 2.2). These penetrated all social levels and provided the networks par excellence to assist newcomers in finding employment, housing and fuel. It was only logical that the migrants's who were accepted into these networks also followed the electoral advice of their leaders.

As we have seen at the beginning of this chapter, the breakthrough of the Welfare Party in 1994-1995 not only caused widespread panic within Turkey's secular establishment, but also led to vigorous intervention by the military. After the fall of Erbakan and the dissolution of the Welfare Party one year later, its parliamentarians reorganised themselves in the so-called Virtue Party. Against all expectations, they did relatively badly during the national elections of April 1999. They failed to mobilise the anger among the old Welfare Party's supporters and ended up in third place. This poor showing ultimately led to the long-awaited split within the Islamic movement of the National Vision. The old guard, Necmettin Erbakan's circle, was heavily dominated by members of the Nakşibendi brotherhood and stuck to a very religiously-coloured manifesto (sect. 2.2.4). When the Virtue Party was also banned in June 2001, it re-emerged as the Felicity Party. The younger party leaders, including Recep Tayyip Erdoğan (the former mayor of greater Istanbul) and Abdullah Gül, saw this as a dead-end road – both because they realised that a strictly Islamic party would never be accepted as a governing party by the state apparatus (the lesson of February 1997), and because they expected such a party to cater for not more than about twenty per cent of the Turkish electorate. In August 2001, therefore, they launched the Justice and Development Party (*Adalet ve Kalkınma Partisi* or AK Party). It deliberately presented itself as a broad conservative party that respected Islamic standards and values but eschewed an explicitly religious manifesto. The 'Justice' part of the name specifically recalled the Justice Party, the broad conservative people's party which, as a right-wing popular party between 1961 and 1980, had taken over the torch from Menderes' Democratic Party.

During the Islamist breakthrough of 1994-1995, a countermovement had meanwhile developed. While the fall of Erbakan had, to a large extent, been the work of the military leadership, in the following years the military also instigated a broad civil *Atatürkçülük* movement ('atatürkism'). This defensive movement believed that the nation's security was threatened by militant Islam and Kurdish separatism, which in turn were seen to be manipulated by dark 'foreign forces' intent on dividing Turkey. Its supporters expected the state, and in particular the military, to come to their 'rescue'. They also continued to demand measures to defend secularism.

The Atatürkçülük movement's attitude towards democracy and human rights is ambivalent. To prevent the threat of an Islamic takeover or Turkey's fragmentation, its supporters rely on a 'strong state', and are generally willing to accept limitations to democratic rights. They are quick to qualify pluriformity as a weakness (Yavuz 2003: 263). Atatürkists of this persuasion are often convinced that Islam, unlike Christianity, cannot be domesticated within a democratic secular system. Among all their larger, and more active civil organisations, the most outspoken ones were (and are) the Association of Atatürkist Thought (*Atatürkçü Düşünce Derneği*) and the Associate for Support for Contemporary Life (*Çağdaş Yaşamı Destekleme Derneği*). The supporters of this civil atatürkism took a very dim view of the 12 September 1980 coup and its legacy, the spread of the Turkish-Islamist Synthesis. The junta of 1980 is seen as a group of 'false Kemalists' who invited fundamentalism in through the backdoor (Erdoğan in Yerasimos et al. (ed.) 2000: 251-2; 277-8).

Interestingly, both the Islamists and the Atatürkists employ an opposition discourse. Each movement views itself as the weaker party fighting for a good cause. The Islamists consider themselves the victims of an omnipotent and unjust state, whereas the Atatürkists believe that Atatürk's legacy has been squandered and that 'real' Atatürkists no longer have access to political power (Erdoğan in Yerasimos et al. (ed.) 2000: 251-2; 261-2).

During the years of Kemalist restoration after February 1997, and certainly after the 1999 elections, state-oriented secularists in Turkey appeared to be winning, but internal conflicts in the ruling coalition in 2002 made fresh elections inevitable. These elections caused a political landslide. The earlier mentioned AK Party received more than 34 per cent of the vote which, due to the idiosyncrasies of the Turkish electoral system, translated into two-thirds of the parliamentary seats. This victory was so overwhelming that it had become impossible to form a government without the inclusion of the AK Party. It was a *fait accompli* that the state apparatus also accepted.

Since the 2002 elections and the coming to power of the AK Party under Erdoğan, a bipolar system has been operational in Turkey. The state and the governing party each have a fundamentally different notion of secularism. Supported by the secularist opposition and Atatürkist civil movements, the state seeks to associate itself with the traditions of the 1930s and 1940s, when secularism was seen as a barrier to safeguard liberty against Islamic forces. The governing party, in turn, associates itself much more with the traditions of Menderes, Demirel and Özal (founder of the Motherland Party in 1983). It believes that a secular state should also provide room for religious individuals to express their standards and values.

At the moment, recovery from the deep financial and economic crisis of 2001 and attempts to obtain EU membership mean that state and politics have a common interest in making their marriage-of-convenience work. The AK Party in particular has a lot to gain from pushing through the reforms needed to fulfil the EU's Copenhagen criteria. After all, these reforms tend to transfer state power to actors in society. However, there are constant irritations endangering this symbiosis. These tend to flare up in connection with phenomena that have assumed a symbolic value during the Republic's history of secularisation – questions such as dress codes (and the banning of the headscarf) in education and within the state apparatus, on which fierce political debates has raged over the last twenty years (Göle 1996).

2.2 OFFICIAL DOCTRINE VERSUS TARIKATS AND NEO-MOVEMENTS

2.2.1 MYSTICAL ORDERS AND CURRENT AFFAIRS

Turkish mystical Islamic brotherhoods (*tarikats*) were dissolved and banned in 1925, and their properties transferred to the state. And yet there is something odd about them. Whoever wants to visit, for example, the tomb of the holy mystic Celaleddin Rumi in Konya, can happily go there as a tourist – with pleasure, since the complex is a museum that falls under the authority of the Turkish Ministry of Culture. Once inside, the visitor will notice that countless Turkish visitors, mainly women, are actually on pilgrimage. Devotion and commerce seem to go hand in hand on this spot. Both Rumi texts and Rumi trinkets are for sale in and around the museum, and there are regular tourist performances of *Mevlevi*-Dervish's ritual dances in for instance the local sports hall. In places like this, signs of devotion are omnipresent – votive offerings are left and visitors can sometimes be found in a state of ecstasy, wandering around with tears in their eyes (Shankland 1999: 67).

113

Almost eighty years after their abolition, the various mystical orders still make the news on an almost daily basis. Especially since the mid-1990s, the newspapers are full of alarming reports on the activities of religious networks, in particular on their infiltration of the state apparatus. This raises the question of how the Dervish orders managed to survive Turkey's secularisation measures and what role they play in the current Islamic landscape.

2.2.2 ISLAMIC MYSTICISM

Islam, like Judaism, is first and foremost a system of standards, values and rules, of which Muslims believe they have been revealed by God. Living according to the commandments of God's law (the şeriat) is the first requirement for a true believer. However, early in the history of Islam there also emerged the need for a more direct, personal and emotional religious experience that went beyond the mere following of God's law. Thus, Islamic mysticism (*tassavuf* or Sufism) was born. The aim of the mystic is to go beyond the şeriat in order to experience divine reality (*hakikat*) in a personal way. Mystics call the individual's path towards this aim, which runs along many intermediate stages, the *tarikat* (path).

Wandering mystical preachers and holy men played a leading role during the conversions to Islam of the Turkish peoples of Western Central Asia, and even before the start of migration to the Middle East. These mystics have remained influential among the Turks. Their popularity was also partially due to their use of everyday language rather than the Arabic of scholarly Islam.

During the era of severe crisis in the Middle East caused by the Mongol incursions and the Crusades (1200-1300 AD), Islamic mysticism actually blossomed. It also underwent organisational changes. Whereas previously mystics were mostly engaged with their faith on an individual basis or in small groups, there now began to emerge personalities who were recognized as a master (*mürşid* or *şeyh*, or 'sheikh') by large groups of followers. While the majority of these sheikhs had no intention whatsoever of establishing a school, their followers gradually organised themselves in mystical orders or brotherhoods, and their teachers came to be regarded as founders. Over time, the word *tarikat* obtained popularity to refer to the brotherhoods that considered themselves the spiritual descendents of one and the same teacher. It is in this sense that is used in Turkey to this day.

2.2.3 THE TARIKATS AND THE OTTOMAN STATE

The Ottoman Empire was home to many Sufi orders. Some of them had their origins in Central Asia, others in Anatolia or the Arab world. They all placed a much higher value on intuitive insight into divine truth (*marifet*) than on religious knowledge obtained by learning (*ilim*). Nevertheless, both the mystics themselves and their followers considered it important to demonstrate that mysticism in no way conflicts with orthodox Sunni teachings, even if the lifestyles and rituals of some mystics or brotherhoods suggests otherwise.

The mystic who wants to achieve unity with God, can do so through self-denial and absolute devotion to God, a process which requires passing through several stages or levels. All brotherhoods are also aware of their own specific spiritual and physical exercises aimed at accelerating this unification process. These are called *zikir*, literally: 'the commemoration' (of God's name). Zikir can take various shapes and forms, from a simple repetition, in silence or not, of the first part of the profession of faith ('There is no god but God/Allah') to the renowned music and dance of the Mevlevi Dervishes (Buitelaar & Ter Haar (eds.) 1999: 9-17).

The *tarikats* played a very important role in the Ottoman Empire as channels between the urban and rural population and the state. The leaders of local Dervish monasteries (*tekkes*) often had great authority, allowing them to solve local conflicts through mediation. In societies in which the cultural, power and wealth gaps between the governing elites and the people were not only massive, but also constantly emphasised as core elements of the 'world order', the brotherhoods provided one of the few channels that cut straight through the social strata. The vast majority of tarikat members were not 'full-time mystics' but lay brothers who combined their membership with a social function, varying from porter, shopkeeper or professional soldier to governor. Many religious scholars were simultaneously also mystics (Zürcher 1993: 14). Hierarchy within the order, which was based on the individual's acquired level of mystical enlightenment and insight, could thus cut across a social hierarchy based on position and status.

The Ottoman sultans systematized and organised the brotherhoods, as they had done before when they incorporated all the ulema into an hierarchical, controlled system previously unknown to the Middle East. The paradox that we have encountered in official Ottoman Islam, also applied to the mystic brotherhoods – the Ottomans incorporated the brotherhoods into the state apparatus in a way that gave the rulers some control, but also allowed for a growing influence of these brotherhoods on not just the state, but also the capital (Mardin 1989: 183-5). The sultans themselves, as well as many of the highest state functionaries, openly associated themselves with one or more of the tarikats. In every major town, a 'head of the brotherhoods' (şeyh al-turuk) was appointed, whom the state held responsible for the conduct of the organised mystics (Geoffroy in EI2, vol. X: 243-6).

The 19th century Ottoman sultans, from Mahmut II (r. 1808-1839) to Abdülhamit II (r. 1876-1909), primarily took on the role of champions of Sunni orthodoxy, but they also understood that the mystic brotherhoods were essential for creating broad social support among the masses. Sufi sheiks were actively used by the court for propaganda purposes, but state control over their activities remained pivotal. Sultan Mahmut's creation of a Ministry for Pious Foundations had the specific purpose of controlling the appointments of local tekke sheikhs (Abu Manneh 1979: 138; Deringil 1998: 63-6).

In the 19th and early 20th century, the mystical brotherhoods seemed to have increased their influence and popularity even further. This can be interpreted as part of the Islamic reaction to Europe's economic, political and cultural penetration in that period (Zürcher 1993: 200). It has also been pointed out that the reforms of the Ottoman Empire and the Kemalist Republic during this period actually depersonalised the traditional patrimonial system based on personal relationships between patron and client, and replaced this by a formal, Western-style contractual relationship. It was only within the networks of orders, where personal connections between master and pupil were pivotal, that these old codes remained intact (Mardin 1989: 10-13).

2.2.4 THE NAKŞIBENDI ORDER

Of all the Sufi brotherhoods in operation during the Ottoman Empire and the Turkish Republic, the Nakşibendi order undoubtedly played the most important role. It went all the way back to 14th century, where Bahaeddin Nakşbend lived in Bukhara, present-day Uzbekistan. During the 15th and 16 centuries, his order spread through all of Central Asia, even reaching the Indian subcontinent. In India in the 18th century, the order gave birth to a movement for renewal, which reached the Ottoman Empire through the preachings of Mevlana Khalid Baghdadi (1776-1827).

Inspired by these events in India, Khalid introduced two significant reforms that became charcteristic to the *Nakşibendi* movement in the Ottoman Empire: the compulsory retreat for novices and the doctrine of the *rabita*, the unbreakable spiritual bond between the master and his pupil. Clearly, these changes considerably assisted discipline and cohesion within the order. The *Khalidi* version of the *Nakşibendi* doctrine soon became dominant in the regions under Ottoman control. It placed itself emphatically on the side of Sunni orthodoxy and stressed the importance of obedience to the rules of the holy law. One could also say this highly influential Dervish order was directed against the Western-style reforms of the Tanzimat era (1839-1871) and against the later reforms of the Young Turks. Instead, it was closely linked to the Islamist policies of Sultan Abdülhamit II (Zarcone in EI2, vol. X: 332-4).

2.2.5 KEMALIST ACTION AGAINST THE ORDERS

On 30 November 1925, two years after the declaration of the Republic of Turkey, the parliament in Ankara decided, under law 677, to abolish the Dervish orders. Its centres, the *tekkes*, were closed and transferred to the state. This decision was primarily dictated by the anticlericalism of the Kemalists, for whom the mystical sheikhs, even more than the ulema, symbolised the nation's backwardness. Another reason was undoubtedly the fact that their widespread networks, with their close-knit structures and culture of obedience to the authority of religious leaders, provided competing power bases that the Kemalist state refused to tolerate.

The orders had no other choice but to close down, resist or go underground. Resistance there was, especially in the early years of the Republic, but this was limited to more isolated incidents. Some of these incidents, such as the murder of reserve officer Kubilay in Menemen in 1930, were seized upon to pursue large-scale persecutions, in this case of the Nakşibendis. Going underground was much easier for some orders than for others. The Nakşibendis, members of the most common Dervish order, had a relatively easy time since they did not employ elaborate rituals involving song and dance, and could also convene in private living rooms. Several of their branches thus survived the Kemalist one-party dictatorship (1925-1945) without too many problems. Their main branche was the *İskenderpaşa* community in Istanbul, led by Sheikh Mehmed Zahid Kotku (1897-1980). As the 'spiritual father' of the National Vision movement, he became active in Turkish politics at the ends of the 1960s, under his pupil Necmettin Erbakan. After Kotku's death, the community was led by his son-in-law, Mehmed Esat Coşan, who fled to Australia after the February 1997 military intervention, where he also died in 2001. His son and successor after his death, Muharrem Nurettin Coşan, still leads this influential and thriving branch of the Nakşibendi order (Yavuz 2003: 139-142).

A key survival strategy of the Nakşibendis during the years of rampant Kemalist secularism was their active lobbying for functions in the bureaucracy of the Directorate of Religious Affairs, the Diyanet. Several obtained influential positions, which they could exploit when the Democratic Party's 1950 victory brought more tolerance for religious expression. Although Menderes did not repeal the ban on the Dervish orders (nor did any of his successors), by the mid-1950s, the mystic sheikhs could increasingly publicly guide their followers, if not unwatched by the bastions of secularism – the military, the public prosecutor's office and the judiciary.

117

As with all the large Dervish orders, the Nakşibendi order over the years split into various subbranches. Currently, there are five branches in Turkey that consider themselves part of the order and are also recognised as such by the other branches. Aside from the earlier mentioned İskenderpaşa community, the *Erenköy* community is also highly influential. There are, however, many others that owe much of their philosophies to the Nakşibendi order, but no longer qualify as part of it. This brings us into the realm of the 'neo-movements' or 'neo-*tarikats*'. Three of these deserve a separate treatment: the *Nurcu* movement (Disciples of the Light), the *Süleymancıs* (Disciples of Süleyman), and the *Fethullahcılar* (followers of Fethullah), whose movement evolved out of the Nurcu movement.

2.2.6 SAIT NURSÎ AND THE NURCU MOVEMENT

Sait Nursî (1876-1960), called Bediüzzaman (Wonder of the Age) by his followers, was a Kurdish Nakşibendi. He came from a village community and had little or no formal education. Nursî had had an ambivalent relationship with the Young Turks. He had taken part in the counterrevolution of 1909, but had also served as a propagandist for the government in the First World War. He had supported Mustafa Kemal Pasja's national resistance movement, but had already warned against secularist tendencies in

1923. Prior to 1908 he had built up a reputation as a religious scholar, particularly in the southeast of Anatolia. After the Kurdish 'Sheikh Sait Uprising' of 1925, along with many other prominent Kurds, he was arrested and deported to the town of Isparta in the west of the country. Since the 1920s, he had begun to record his religious ideas in books and pamphlets, which later became known as the *Risale-i Nur – Külliyatı ('Message of the Light – Collected Works')*. In his work he called upon Muslims to make God's indivisibility the foundation of their lives, but he also urged them to study and employ modern Western science and technology to further the cause of Islam. Since he saw the Muslim community as the only true basis for social cohesion, he rejected nationalism. A large part of his work consisted of calls to use in-depth-study of the Koran as a stepping stone from which to reform and adapt Islam to the needs of the modern age, thus facilitating its use in the fight against materialism and positivism (Yavuz 2000: 7, 14). The collected statements of Sait Nursî took many directions, were often obscure or multi-interpretable, but that merely increased their appeal to a wide range of different groups (Karpat in EI2, vol. VIII: 143-4).

Between 1935 and 1953, Sait Nursî was arrested several times and tried for the political use of religion, but while he did preach social mobilisation and rejected both secularism and nationalism, he did not directly involve himself in political matters. His writings were banned during the Kemalist period, but they were copied out by hand by his ever wider circle of disciples. Under Menderes, whom he increasingly supported throughout the 1950s, he was given more breathing space for his preaching. Secularists, however, considered his public support for only one political party as an horrendous example of the political abuse of religion. After his death in 1960, the *Nurcu* movement, as it was now called, continued to grow. It became influential both in Turkey itself and amongst Turkish immigrants in European countries (Zürcher 1993: 201).

Sait Nursî did not look upon his movement as a tarikat in the classic sense of the word and he did not seen himself as a sheikh, but as an imam (Karpat in EI2, vol. VIII: 143-4). Indeed, he was not succeeded after his death, as would have been the case with a true Dervish order. Instead, the written account of his message, the *Risale*, has become the centrepiece of his rapidly expanding community of followers. Due to the importance of this text for their movement, the Nurcus have also applied themselves successfully to printing and publishing.

The political differences in the Turkey during the 1970s and 1980s also led to schisms within the Nurcu movement. When, in 1970, the first true Islamist party (Erbakan's National Order Party, later National Salvation Party) was formed by members of the İskenderpaşa movement, several

Nurcus gave it their support, while the majority remained loyal to Süleyman Demirel's Justice Party. A more serious schism occurred on the occa-
sion of the military coup d'état in September 1980. The military were
supported by a few prominent Nurcu leaders, such as Mehmet Kırkıncı in
Erzurum and Fethullah Gülen in Izmir, but they were fiercely opposed by a
group called *Yeni Asya* ('New Asia', a newspaper), which continued to
support deposed prime minister Demirel. In the early 1980s, this split
eventually gave rise to two new branches, one supporting Turgut Özal and
his Motherland Party, and the other supporting Demirel, who had meanwhile been banned from politics. However, politics was not the only factor
behind these splits in the Nurcu movement. There are currently ten different Nurcu movements, with ideas ranging from the extremely fundamentalist to the modernist (Yavuz 2003: 179).

2.2.7 THE SÜLEYMANCIS

The founder of the second large Islamic 'neo-movement' in Turkey, Süleyman Hilmi Tunahan (1888-1959), was both a Nakşibendi sheikh and a
conservative religious scholar. Already in the 1930s and 1940s, when the
Republic had abolished all formal religious education, Tunahan had made
an effort to offer Islamic instruction. Since this was of course illegal, he had
frequent encounters with the police.

Tunahan and his followers primarily concentrated on the Koranic schools.
In 1949, when the Kemalist regime's democratisation efforts meant that
Koranic schools were officially allowed to operate again, the Süleymancis
readily seized their chance. With 25 years of experience, they were well-
placed to train religious functionaries for positions in the bureaucracy of
the Directorate of Religious Affairs. In the 1950s and 1960s, as growing
prosperity in the countryside was accompanied by an explosive rise in the
number of mosques, many newly appointed preachers were indeed graduates of Tunahan's schools. The Süleymancis and the state developed a
symbiotic relationship; the Süleymancis incorporated nationalism and
respect for the state firmly into their Islamic teaching, while the state in
turn tried to used their movement as a potential counterweight to the ever-
present communist threat.

The 'intimate' relationship between the Süleymancis and the state was
disrupted after 1965. A new law for the Directorate of Religious Affairs
declared that only graduates of official schools for preachers could be
appointed. After the March 1971 military 'coup by memorandum', in which
the army extracted several far-reaching changes in legislation, many of the
Süleymancı's private schools were taken over by the state. The resulting
coolness in their relationship with the state also prompted the Süleymancis

to explore new spheres of activity, which they found in the provision of Islamic education to the increasingly large Turkish communities in Europe. The Directorate of Religious Affairs had neglected the spiritual needs of Turkish migrants in Europe, and so the Süleymancıs were fulfilling a real need.

After the military takeover of September 1980, the Directorate was given the task of propagating the state-sympathetic Islam of the Turkish-Islamic Synthesis among the Turks in Europe. This led to the restoration of the warm relationship between the Directorate and the Süleymancıs, and allowed the latter even more room to manoeuvre. Today, the movement runs a large network of boarding schools, especially in Germany. These use the latest technology for the teaching and indoctrination of their pupils (Yavuz 2003: 146-7). Discipline plays a key role. In line with the Khalidi tradition we mentioned earlier, Süleyman Tunahan emphasised the direct spiritual bond between the teacher (i.e. himself) and his followers. His personality cult still plays an important role within the movement. Tunahan is seen as the last and most perfect of holy men. Having visions of the sheikh and becoming absorbed into them, is considered a prerequisite for knowledge of divine reality (Yavuz 2003: 145-7).

2.2.8 THE FETHULLAHCILAR

A movement which shares the Süleymancı's emphasis on education, is that of the followers of *Hoca* (teacher) Fethullah Gülen, born in a village near Erzurum, northeast Turkey, in 1941. This movement originates from the Nurcu movement, but it has developed an entirely own identity over the last ten years.

Fethullah Gülen, at first a follower of the Nurcu movement, began his career as a preacher in a mosque in Izmir, but found his calling in arranging accommodation, or boarding-houses, for poor, Islamic-oriented pupils and students. From this start, he built up an education network of Summer camps and intensive courses preparing for state exams. Like Tunahan, he offered a cheap alternative to the expensive private schools used by the urban middle classes to give their offspring a good start in life. Over the years, countless pupils from impoverished backgrounds got the chance to pursue a career in Turkey's enormous administrative bureaucracy. This was and is exactly the sort of 'infiltration' which greatly worries the army and the secular middle class (Shankland 1999: 83-5).

Unlike the Süleymancıs, Fethullah and his followers have also built up a large network of institutions for further and higher education. The liberalisation of Turkish education since 1983, allowed for the starting of grammer schools and universities run by foundations rather than by the state. The movement immediately jumped on this development and now, twenty years later, it administers over two hundred schools for further education as well as seven universities. These are not just based in Turkey, but also in Western Europe (e.g. the Islamic University of Rotterdam), in the Balkans and in Central Asia.

Like other branches of the Nurcu movement, Fethullah Gülen attached great importance to developing his own media. At first, he concentrated on the printed media, such as the daily newspaper *Zaman* (The Times), but the deregulation of Turkish radio and television also enabled him to launch private radio and television stations. The best known is his television station *Samanyolu* (Milky Way).

Gülen's rise certainly benefited from the fact that, from the start, he strongly backed the military coup of September 1980. With the assistance of the then prime minister, and later president, Turgut Özal, who himself had strong connections with the Nakşibendi order, Gülen presented himself as the spokesman for a modern, forward-looking, and state-sympathetic Islam. The symbiosis of the Fethullahcılar and the state remained intact for a long time. In the mid-1990s, Fethullah Gülen was still generally seen by the political establishment as the 'acceptable face of Islam', and politicians across the spectrum, from the right (Tansu Çiller) to the left (Bülent Ecevit) praised him and met him publicly. Gülen also supported the military intervention of February 1997, also when this eventually led to the fall of the Erbakan government. He criticised Erbakan's Welfare Party, describing it as radical.

Despite all such attempts at portraying his movement as a pillar under the state, the military eventually also came down on Fethullah's movement. This scenario perfectly fitted the u-turn of Turkey's secularist, pro-state movements since the mid-1990s, and it also opened the debate on the entire legacy of the 1980 coup, including Islam's incorporation into the state ideology. In June 1999, the Turkish media, under directions from the National Security Council, began a fierce campaign against Gülen. They reported the 'discovery' of tapes with recordings of sermons of 1986, in which he called on his followers to be patient and to infiltrate the state organs from below. The Chief of the General Staff spoke openly about Gülen's plans to undermine the state, and in 2000 Gülen was formally accused of attempting to alter the secular character of the Republic. Fethullah Gülen thereafter went into exile in the United States, where he still is today (Yavuz 2003: 183, 202-3; Shankland 1999: 83-5).

2.2.9 FINANCING OF THE ORDERS: FOUNDATIONS AND ASSOCIATIONS

Almost eighty years since the original banning of the Dervish orders in Turkey, they are still illegal in the eyes of the law. However, since the 1950s and even more so since the 1980s, both the religious orders and the neo-movements have managed to set up an immense network of schools, publishers, television stations, hospitals and other kinds of services. These institutions have nearly always taken on the legal form of charitable foundations (*vakıf*), and they are maintained with voluntary contributions. Support for these foundations is often organised in associations (*dernek*). Since the late 1980s, many of the financial contributions to these networks have come from Islamic businessmen. The liberalisation of the Turkish economy has mobilised a whole new class of, often highly prosperous, entrepreneurs in the provincial Anatolian towns. These are people who tend to combine strict religious ideas with modern entrepreneurship and a predilection for technology. The best-known example of this is Kombasan, an industrial conglomerate in Konya, which has recently been accused of supporting fundamentalist movements in Turkey with investments obtained under false pretexts from Turks elsewhere in Europe. This combination of money, a tightly-knit organisation and targeted indoctrination through education is seen by secular circles in Turkey as the single largest threat to their country's Western orientation.

2.3 SUNNI ISLAM AND ALEVISM

2.3.1 THE NON-SUNNI MOVEMENTS

The previous paragraphs have stressed the varied nature of Islam in Turkey, which is expressed in, for instance, the relationship between state-Islam and mystical brotherhoods and neo-movements. While these all belong to Sunni Islam, this should not lead to the impression that Turkey is a uniformly Sunni nation. On the contrary, apart from the 80 to 85 per cent Sunni majority, the country is also home to important heterodox groupings. Turkey thus reflects the situation within the Muslim world at large.

The large majority of Muslims in the world, some 85 per cent, adhere to the Sunni faith, but there are a few dozen other creeds and persuasions in Islam. The best-known is that of the Shia, more specifically the so-called 'Twelver' Shiites, a name which points to the fact that its followers recognise twelve rightful successors to the prophet Mohammed. It is the state religion of Iran and the religion of the majority of Iraqis. Of the smaller other creeds within Islam, several others belong to Shia, but not to the Iranian variety. Again others have clear similarities to Shia, but their followers are not recognised as co-religionists by the majority of Shiites.

Examples are the Druses of Syria and Lebanon, the *ehl-i haqq* and *yezidis* ('devil-worshippers') of Kurdistan and the Alevis of Turkey. Since their beliefs are so different from those of mainstream Sunni and Shiite, they are now also widely known in the Middle East by the umbrella term of *ghulât* ('exaggerators') (Douwes in Driessen (ed.) 1997: 162).

In this chapter, we will concentrate on only one of these heterodox groups, the Alevis of Turkey.

2.3.2 WHO ARE THE ALEVIS?

The Alevis are currently the largest religious minority in Turkey. However, it is virtually impossible to provide an accurate assessment of their numbers. The Republic of Turkey recognises no religious minorities other than the Christians and Jews, whose status was internationally established in the Treaty of Lausanne (1923). Most Alevis speak Turkish, while a smaller proportion speaks one of the Kurdish languages. They live scattered over large areas of the country and have no special external features. The Turkish censuses do not register the Alevis; they are simply registered as Muslims. While estimates of their numbers range from ten to twenty million, a twelve to fifteen million-range is perhaps the most realistic (Shindeldecker 2000; Kehl-Bodrogi 1997: XI-XII; Gezik 2000; Shankland 1999: 136).

123

The Turkish Alevis traditionally inhabit a wide belt stretching from Ankara, through Çorum, Yozgat, Amasya, Samsun, Tokat and Sivas, to Erzincan in the east and Kahramanmaraş in the south. Kurdish Alevis predominantly live in the provinces of Bingöl, Elazığ, Tunceli, and Malatya. What holds for the Alevis, however, also holds for the entire rural population of Turkey; due to massive migration into the cities since the 1950s, a large proportion of the population now lives in the immense agglomerations of Istanbul, Izmir, Ankara, Bursa and Adana. Since the regions from which the Alevis originated are among the poorer areas in Turkey, migration levels were even higher there. It is therefore no exaggeration to expect about half of today's Alevis to live in large cities. As we will see, the drift to the cities has had large consequences for Alevi identity.

Historically, modern Alevism originated from the many heterodox groups which, at the start of the 16th century, fell under the spell of the Shiite Safawid movement and that supported the Safawid Shah Ismaïl against the Ottoman sultan. What was basically a political power struggle between Sunni Ottomans and Shiite Safawids, forced the population of Anatolia and Kurdistan to take sides. For the many Anatolian tribes adhering to heterodox, syncretic forms of Islam which included Christian and shamanistic elements, the Safawid movement was much more familiar than the Ottomans, who had by now become sedentary and Sunni.

The Ottomans succeeded in defeating the Safawid movement in Anatolia and the Western Kurdish regions. The Ottoman Sultan Selim I (r. 1512-1520), in particular, organised horrendous pogroms among the Anatolian ghulât. These military conflicts and their consequences, were decisive for the relationship between the Ottoman state and the Alevi minority in the centuries to come. The Alevis could assert themselves in isolated rural areas and, where possible, avoid contact with the state and the Sunni population. Now inward-looking, the Alevi community developed a close-knit social and religious organisation that enabled them to survive in a hostile environment (Ocak 1997). Towards the outside world, the Alevis lived by the principle of *takiye* (prudently concealing one's convictions), which was also accepted in other Shiite creeds.

After the 16th century, Ottoman policies ceased to aim at persecuting Alevi 'heretics' and instead exuded a kind of silent tolerance. Silent, since sectarianism within the community of believers was ideologically unacceptable and nowhere recorded. In theory, the *ümmet*, the Islamic community of faithful, was indivisible. This tolerance did not mean equal justice, though. The Alevis were generally despised by the Sunni majority, which harboured many prejudices against the relatively closed and unknown Alevi community. Traces of this prejudice, particularly in reference to their sexual morality, can still be found today.

Somewhat like the Jewish people, the Alevis survived because religion was also seen as ethnicity. The Alevis considered themselves as a tribal community and maintained strict endogamy. Only those born within the community could receive the knowledge of the Alevi doctrine. This was passed on orally by the *dedes* ('grandfathers') or *pirs* ('spiritual elders'), a sort of hereditary priestly castes that claimed to be descendants of the prophet. The *dedes* also functioned as judges and mediators within the community, thus ensuring as much as possible that community members would appeal to an Ottoman judge (Kehl-Bodrogi 1997: XI-XII).

2.3.3   ARE THE ALEVIS MUSLIMS?

The much-posed question of whether the Alevis can still be considered Muslims, even though their faith and rituals are so different from Sunni orthodoxy, is answered very differently in Sunni and Alevi communities. The most meaningful way of reaching a conclusion, without passing judgment (since one man's religion is another man's sect), is by comparing Alevi religious ideas and principles with those of Sunni and 'twelver' Shiite Islam.

In all three branches of Islam, the so-called 'Five Pillars' are seen as basic obligations of the faith:
1 professing the faith;
2 fasting;
3 ritual praying;
4 giving alms to the poor;
5 undertaking the pilgrimage to Mecca.

Using this checklist, we can establish the following differences.

1 Professing the faith
Everyone who wants to become a Muslim must solemnly profess: "There is no god but God/Allah and Mohammed is God's messenger". Alevis also profess this, but it is not clear to what extent this is a form of *takiye*. Some Alevis add: "And Ali is the proconsul of God and the confident of Mohammed." This emphasises the enormous importance that Alevis, and other Shiites, attach to the person of Ali, the son-in-law and cousin of the prophet. They see him as the first Muslim, the only rightful successor to Mohammed who was sidelined by 'impostors' after the prophet's death. Some even go so far as to assume that God's revelations were intended for Ali, not Mohammed. In Alevi religious practice, Ali fulfils a larger and also more sentimental role than Mohammed.

In Alevi thought, there is also a large role for the concept of the good or complete person (*insan*), of whom Ali is the prototype. This also brings a sense of perspective to the faith itself, by assuming that what is important is not religion, but being a (good) person. Modern Alevi writers therefore often compare their creed to European humanism.

2 Fasting
Both Sunni and 'regular' Shiite Muslims fast between sunrise and sunset during the thirty days of the month of *Ramazan* in the Islamic calendar, but Alevis generally do not. Fasts are generally held during twelve days of the month of *Muharrem*, commemorating the death of Ali's youngest son who, along with most of Ali's family, was murdered by opponents in 680 AD.

3 Ritual praying
Devout Muslims perform the ritual prayer (*namaz*), a combination of strictly regulated movements and utterances, five times a day. Attending Friday afternoon prayer, including the weekly sermon, is in principle an obligation for all men. Alevis do neither. In Alevi villages, traditionally there are also no mosques, although attempts were made, both under the late Ottoman Empire and the Republic, to 'Sunni-fy' the Alevis by erecting

mosques in their villages and districts. The Republic undertook this after 1980, when the Turkish-Islamic Synthesis, with its mixed religious-nationalist message, became the state ideology.

Alevis have their own religious gatherings or services. This is the *ayini cem* (gathering), which traditionally takes place on Thursday evening. Held in a purpose-built place or a normal house, it is led by a *dede*, who on such occasions also hears disputes, reconciles people and can also impose punishments. His most severe sanction is a form of excommunication (*düşkünlük*), an eviction from the community, which in the old days of isolated Anatolian villages obviously amounted to a death penalty. The confession of sins and the communal meal, which may well have been adopted from Christian sacraments, form part of the service in which both men and women participate. In Alevi rituals, ballads to the accompaniment of a lute, often on the subject of the death of Ali and his sons, occupy a major place.

4 Giving alms to the poor
The Alevis have a strong tradition of donating to charitable causes for the benefit of the community, but this is not done according to the detailed rules of Sunni Islam.

5 Undertaking the pilgrimage to Mecca
The Alevis are not in the habit of making the pilgrimage to Mecca, but they often pay their respects to the tombs of Alevi saints in Anatolia. This has the purpose of spiritual cleansing, not of obtaining a place in paradise. The best known pilgrimage takes place on 16 August, leading to the grave of Haci Bektaş, founder of the *Bektaşi* Dervish order which is related to Alevism. Prior to 1925, this order was widespread, but it now mainly lives on in Albania. The exact relationship between the more urbanised and educated members of the *Bektaşi* order and the oral traditions of the Alevis, has long been the subject of scholarly debate.

From the above, one could conclude that the Alevis are indeed very far removed from the mainstream of Islam, but still fall under the category of (Shiite) Islam. This is a lot less clear in the case of other 'ghulât communities', such as the Druzses and the Yezedis. Drawing a comparison with Christianity again, we could perhaps say that Sunnis and Alevis are all Muslims, just as Roman Catholics and Quakers are all Christians.

2.3.4 ALEVIS AND KEMALISM

Various modern Alevi authors claim a central role for their community in the birth of the independence movement (Şener 1991: 12), but this is a gross exaggeration. It is true that most Alevis in Anatolia aligned themselves with Mustafa Kemal Pasja and his national movement during the Turkish war of independence (1919-1922). Event though this movement fought emphatically in the name of the sultan-caliph (Zürcher in Karpat (ed.) 2000: 150-79), Mustafa Kemal expressly sought their support. Even so, there were tribes, mainly Kurdish and Alevi, who resisted the authority of Ankara. Their resistance was largely inspired by their aversion to the central state's attempts to establish actual control over the tribes in the mountainous regions of East Anatolia, which until then had been practically autonomous.

Their memories of suppression by the Ottoman state, and their position as a mistrusted marginal group within the Sunni caliphate (which had been in the hands of Ottoman sultans for centuries), made the Alevis natural allies of the Kemalist reformers. These reformers, after all, deprived Sunni Islam of its dominant role in public life (Aydın 2000: 16-26). While state and society under the Republic remained dominated by Sunni Muslims, the radical secularism and anticlericalism of the Kemalist regime to some extent rid the state of its hostile image among the Alevi's. They were prepared to accept that the Republic did not recognise them as a religious community, as long as that same Republic would deny all forms of religion a place in the public sphere. In the Republic, takiye remained a way of life for the Alevis, but they obtained better opportunities for social mobility (Kehl-Bodrogi 1997: XII-XIII).

The love affair between the state and the Alevis was, to some extent, reciprocal. Much to their disappointment, the order of the Bektaşi, who were related by faith to the Alevi, was not exempted from the ban on Dervish orders, yet its legacy was judged in a positive light. The Ministry of Education even published an anthology of Bektaşi poets, and their poems were praised as examples of 'real' Turkish culture (Birge 1937: 17). During the process of nation-building based on a Turkish national identity, the Alevis were also identified as a people who, during the Ottoman era, when elite culture was completely dominated by Arabic and Persian languages and cultures, had held on to the Turkish language and had thus preserved Turkish culture from demise (Shankland 1993: 175; Poulton 1997: 126). The equal status of women in Alevi and Bektaşi culture was also singled out and interpreted as a continuation of old Turkish traditions, to which the modern Republic now reconnected (Poulton 1997: 126-7).

At the same time, some of the worst armed conflicts of the 1930s were fought between the Kemalist Republic's troops and Alevi groups. When the state wanted to impose its authority upon the vast and highly isolated mountain region of Dersim, Alevi Kurdish tribes rebelled and were brutally suppressed. In the aftermath of this rebellion, large numbers of Dersim's inhabitants were deported to the West and Middle of Anatolia, where their descendents still live.

2.3.5 URBAN MIGRATION

For centuries, the Alevis essentially formed a rural community that had managed to continue its existence in physical and social isolation by limiting contacts with the outside world as much as possible. In such an environment, oral traditions, supported by the authority of the dedes, provided the community with structure and a sense of purpose. Since the mid-1950s, however, Turkey experienced the twin processes of agricultural mechanisation and industrialisation. This meant that rural workers made redundant began to move from the countryside to the cities. Still in 1950, eighty per cent of the population lived in the countryside, while in 2000 this figure had dropped to fifty per cent. In this urban, industrialised and anonymous environment, traditional forms of Alevi faith were hard to uphold, as these were based on personal contact (Kehl-Bodrogi 1997: 119-20).

In this new, impersonal environment of the big city, with its daily contacts with the Sunni majority, Alevi newcomers looked for a new base from which to build up their solidarity networks. As with other migrant groups in Turkey, the first generation found this mainly in their *hemşerilik*, their shared local origins. A typical migration organisation, for instance, could be that of the 'Society of People from Sivas'. It would have its own teahouse, centrally located in the district that housed a lot of migrants from Sivas, as well as its own elected board. In the multi-party democracy of the postwar period, this board could effectively use the community's political support to obtain concessions from the city's administrators.

In the late 1960s, Alevism as a religious identity seemed to disappear like snow in summer. Instead, a growing number of mainly younger Alevis interpreted their heritage in political terms. Traditionally, most Alevis were supporters of the Republican People's Party founded by Atatürk, because of its emphasis, in policies and manifestos, on secularism. In the 1960s and 1970s, however, large numbers of Alevi's began opting for radical forms of socialism, with many eventually ending up among the ranks of the extra-parliamentary opposition or even urban guerrilla movements. Alevis were heavily over-represented in all the ultra-left-wing combat groups of the time, whose concept of collective identity considered Alevism as synonymous with communism. They reinterpreted their history as a tale of struggle for justice and against oppression, with leading roles for Ali, Husayn and the Alevi saints. Some explicitly saw Alevism as a form of proto-communism (Van Bruinessen 1996: 8).

Redefining Alevism as a political ideology rather than an ethno-religious identity also led to the failure in the 1960s to transform a separate Alevi political party into the mouthpiece of the Alevi religious community. There were several attempts, though. In 1966, a group of Alevi entrepreneurs founded the *Birlik Partisi*, the Unity Party. This projected itself explicitly as Alevi, but still failed to muster more than a few per cent of the vote in successive elections. For the secularised Alevis, the attractions of left-wing politics were much larger (Yavuz 2003: 67; Kehl-Bodrogi 1997: XIII).

The Alevis' prominent role in ultra-left-wing movements ensured that their opponents (in particular the Sunni ultra-nationalists of the Nationalist Action Party – the so-called 'Idealists' (*Ülkücüler* or 'Grey Wolves')) also adopted the slogan of 'Alevism is communism'. In mobilising their own supporters, such groups thus seized the opportunity to exploit all the existing prejudices about Alevis. During the second half of the 1970s, when Turkey witnessed large social and political tensions, this led to pogroms against Alevis in a whole series of Anatolian towns, such as Tokat, Çankırı, Çorum, Sivas, and Kahramanmaraş. The clashes in Kahramanmaraş in December 1978, were particularly violent, resulting in 106 (mostly Alevi) deaths, and the declaration of the state of emergency in eleven provinces. In July 1980, Sunni extremists again attacked Alevi targets in Çorum, killing 26 people (Yavuz 2003: 68; Poulton 1997: 162).

129

2.3.6 THE REDISCOVERY OF RELIGIOUS ALEVISM

The military coup of September 1980 not merely effectively ended political street-fighting, but also suppressed the ultra-left and socialist movements in which the Alevis had played such a prominent role.

In the 1980s and 1990s, two factors led to a thorough reorientation of the Alevi community. The first was the use of Sunni Islam as an instrument serving state ideology. The introduction of the Turkish-Islamic Synthesis as a semi-official state ideology, and the use (first by the military junta and later by prime minister/president Turgut Özal) of a state-friendly, 'Turkish' Islam to promote social cohesion, alienated Alevis from the state. They felt no longer able to rely on the secular character of the state. Their feelings were bolstered in October 1987, with the return to politics of the 'old' politicians, including the Islamist Erbakan and the ultra-nationalist Türkeş. The victories in 1994-1995 of Erbakan's Welfare Party's and the victory in 1999 of the Nationalist Action Party, seemed to confirm their worst suspicions. In the 1990s, then, the Alevi were among the groups in Turkey who reacted most sharply to the process of Islamisation.

In July 1993, the pressure cooker finally blew. During an Alevi festival in Sivas, an ethnically and religiously very mixed region, a furious crowd of Sunnis attacked a hotel where Alevi poets and singers were staying. The hotel was set alight, resulting in the death of 36 Alevi intellectuals and one Dutch student. What sparked off the violence was a speech by the writer Aziz Nesin (who had also translated Salman Rushdie's *Satanic Verses*), in which he declared that he personally did not believe in the Koran. The Alevis' mistrust of the state increased when it became clear from film footage that the mayor of Sivas had taken part in the demonstration and that the police had hardly intervened. Moreover, the perpetrators, although sentenced by the State Security Court, received reduced sentences for 'having been provoked' (Poulton 1997: 262-3). After the fire in Sivas, several other incidents occurred that were directed against Alevi. In 1994, the Istanbul metropolitan council, then run by the Welfare Party, had an Alevi holy site demolished, and in March 1995, Sunni radicals opened fire on several coffee houses in the Alevi district of Gazi in Istanbul. This led to massive protests throughout the country, in which some thirty people died. Peace was only restored when the Gazi police, who were heavily infiltrated by Grey Wolves, were replaced by military units.

The collapse of the Soviet Union by the end of 1991, and the subsequent crisis this brought upon left-wing movements, was the second factor that prompted Alevis to redefine their identity in ethno-religious rather than political terms. While Turkey's radical movements were generally not loyal to Moscow, and looked for inspiration rather more to Maoism or to the (urban) guerrilla forces of Latin America, the apparent triumph of capitalism and the American victory in the Cold War dealt them a moral blow.

While Alevi reactions to these developments varied, they all reflected a new self-confidence and a deliberate search for publicity – something previously shunned at almost all costs. Already in 1990, several leading Alevi activists had published a manifesto in one of the large, national daily newspapers, asking for the recognition of their community and for freedom of religion. They also increasingly openly voiced their dissatisfaction with the fact that their role as taxpayers meant they automatically contributed to the gigantic bureaucracy of the Directorate of Religious Affairs, which exclusively concerned itself with the Sunni section of the population (Shindeldecker 2000).

The upshot of this Alevi 'coming out' has been a flood of publications, largely from the Alevi side, and also a spectacular rise in the number of Alevi associations. The result is a more visible role for Alevism, both within Turkey and elsewhere Europe. However, this has also revealed the community's fragmentation. This is partly due to the worldwide loss of appeal of various forms of socialism. On a deeper level, it also reflects the problems that Alevis have encountered in their quest for a new sense of purpose in an industrialised, individualised and anonymous urban environment, in which oral traditions and direct contact no longer serve as the main unifying forces of their religious community.

In the current reinterpretation of Alevism, different views coexist. On the one hand, there are some groups who hold on to the interpretation of Alevism as an ethno-religious community, but want to modernise their faith and cleanse it from 'superstition'. For several among these, Alevism is not really a faith at all, but rather a secular value system. Other groups actually make overtures to scriptural, orthodox Islam. A majority of these mirror Turkish Sunni Islam, while a minority take Shii Islam of the Islamic Republic of Iran as their model. Such advances to orthodox strands of Islam also create a need for Alevi theological and sacred texts. It thus seems natural for Alevis to drawn on the writings of the Bektaşi Dervish. For the time being, attempts to model Alevism on the Sunna are very problematical. On the other hand, there are also groups who attempt to preserve the authenticity and unique character of the syncretic Alevi faith, but it is precisely these groups that face extra difficulties in an urban environment (Çamuroğlu in Kehl-Bodrogi (ed.) 1997: 28-9).

More importantly, the bitter struggle in the 1990s between the Turkish army and the Kurdish independence movement (PKK), which took place in a climate of rising ethnic nationalism, put the Alevis in a difficult situation. For a community traditionally made up of both Kurdish and Turkish-speaking members, choosing sides was extremely difficult. However, the brand of nationalism that was propagated, proved so strong that sizeable groups of Kurdish and Turkish Alevis began identifying themselves first and foremost with, respectively, the Kurdish resistance and the Turkish state. Each of these groups also took the political consequences of their respective choices (Çamuroğlu in Kehl-Bodrogi (ed.) 1997: 32).

The *rapprochement* between Turkish nationalists and Alevis was facilitated when the state, in the face of political Islam's breakthrough by the mid-1990s, broke with its Islamic policies of the 1980s. Launched by the military in 1997, this new struggle against political (Sunni) Islam has prompted yet another discourse, this time in secularist circles. This depicts Alevi Islam as 'typically Turkish Islam', and contrasts it with Arab Islam. This implies that Turkish Islam has embraced traditional humanist and emancipatory values, while Arab Islam represents rigidity, narrow-mindedness and fundamentalism (Yavuz 2003: 253). The large, annual Alevi festival around the grave of Haci Bektaş is now recognised by the state, and the state budget now also includes allocations for supporting Alevi associations and for research into Alevism.

2.4 ISLAM, FUNDAMENTALISM AND TERRORISM

2.4.1 TERRORIST ATTACKS

In November 2003, Istanbul was shaken by four suicide attacks, in which 62 people were killed. Two synagogues were attacked, followed five days later by attacks on the British consulate general and a British bank. At first, both Turkish political and public opinion maintained that the culprits were Arabs. This seemed to be confirmed by an e-mail from al-Qaeda claiming responsibility. However, an investigation by the police and the security forces quickly revealed the truth: the culprits were Turkish Kurds from the province of Bingöl, and while they presumably had links to al-Qaeda, they were first and foremost members of their own, Turkey-based organisations.

This event drew both the domestic and international media's attention to the fact that Turkey also has illegal networks of Islamic extremists, and that their presence is not restricted to Arab countries, Pakistan or Indonesia. Islamic extremism, or fundamentalism, is thus part of the landscape of Turkish Islam. But what exactly is Islamic fundamentalism, and how does it differ from other movements within Islam?

2.4.2 MODERNISM, FUNDAMENTALISM AND TRADITIONALISM

At the end of the day, Islam is a text-based community. Like other similar communities such as Christianity or Judaism, it has been confronted throughout the centuries with the dilemma of, on the one hand, the absoluteness of God's will (which, according to Islam, was last revealed to the prophet Mohammed), and on the other hand, the need for continuous reinterpretation. In both classical and modern eras, debates on this dilemma have generally produced three ideal-type positions, often referred to as modernism, fundamentalism and traditionalism.

Modernists, or reformers, advocate a continuous reinterpretation of the moral ideal. Modernists are often motivated by a need to adapt the moral ideal to changing circumstances. Equally often, however, they are driven by the needs of political rulers or opposition groups to manipulate the moral ideal. In this endeavour, modernists emphasise man's moral independence and his freedom and ability to acquire moral knowledge through his own mental abilities. Fundamentalists object to this interpretation of the moral ideal. Their resistance is usually motivated by the desire to protect it from manipulation and corruption by rulers or other politicians intent on using it to justify their political aspirations. Thus, fundamentalists frequently stress the inadequacy and subjectivity of man's moral judgment, which they see as both inevitable and as inevitably reflecting self-interest.

The third position, that of traditionalism, allows for the interpretation of the moral ideal, but once a specific interpretation is provided and subsequently confirmed by agreement among the faithful, it can never be revised. As a result, the authoritative texts of Islam continuously expands with the interpretations of previous generations. Traditionalism is thus a kind of compromise between the two extremes of modernism and fundamentalism. By allowing for interpretation of new cases, and outlawing reinterpretation of old cases, it provides flexibility as well as consistency (Hoebink in Driessen (ed.) 1997: 200-1).

These three positions are easily translated into the reality of the Turkish Islamic landscape. The Young Turkish and Kemalist interpreters of Islam can be seen as modernists. They thought that 'true' Islam was a personal conviction based on reason and open to science. This is why they wanted to making the sources of Islam (through translations in Turkish of the Koran and of sermons) directly accessible to the ordinary faithful. While the main branches of the Nurcu movement can also be seen as modernist, its broad character means that there are some groups, such as the Aczmendi movement, which have drastically shifted towards a fundamentalist view, and which seek to model society on the Community of Mohammed.

133

The orthodox Nakşibendi Dervishes and the National Vision movement that developed from these, are perhaps best classified as traditionalist. This was precisely its appeal to the small businessmen (*esnaf*) who formed the original support base for Erbakan's party. The National Vision movement has obtained a lot of political and social power since the 1970s, but its intellectual contribution to a renewed Islamic élan has ultimately been very small. Traditionalism, though, is not a monolith. In the Netherlands, for instance, the Amsterdam branch of National Vision, under the leadership of Haci Karacaer, has turned itself into a forum for progressive ideas on the male role within the family and on homosexuality. Ideologically, this branch has thus drifted off from the mainstream of Milli Görüş in Europe and Turkey.

The mammoth organisation of the Directorate of Religious Affairs accommodates both (moderate) modernists and traditionalists. In Turkey, real fundamentalists can be found in several relatively small but tightly-knit and active movements. These are people who reject reinterpretation and adaptation of the moral ideal, and who consider the source texts of Islam (the Koran and traditions of the life of the prophet Mohammed) as absolutely valid and literally true. While the latter is also endorsed by many 'ordinary' Muslims, fundamentalists conclude from this that life in Islamic society must be lived according to the letter of God's revelation. Characteristic of such groups is their demand that Islamic holy law, the şeriat, should serve as the only basis for the country's political and legal system. In their view, the holy law must be enforced at all costs, by force if necessary (Jansen 1998: 23-5).

Clearly, their views directly go against the political order and legal system of the Turkish Republic. It will also be obvious from the previous paragraphs that their ideas completely break with Ottoman tradition, which had indeed never assigned a *de facto* central role to the holy law. It goes without saying that agitation for fundamentalist concepts is strictly forbidden in Turkey. Each of the movements discussed below are thus illegal.

2.4.3   IBDA-C

İslami Büyük Doğu Akıncıları – Cephe (Commandoes of the Islamic Great Eastern Front, or IBDA-C) has its roots in the mid-1970s, when a radical faction broke away from the youth movement of Necmettin Erbakan's National Salvation Party. At the time, his party had carried responsibilities of government in several coalition government. In the eyes of these radicals, he had thus betrayed his ideals by being part of a 'corrupt' Turkish regime.

IBDA members derive many of their ideas from the writings of the Turkish author and poet Necip Fazıl Kısakürek (1905-1983). Necip Fazıl was one of the few Islamic thinkers who, during the Kemalist Republic days, clearly voiced their opposition to the development model of Atatürk and his supporters. Against kemalist notions of embracing contemporary Western civilisation, he argues that Islam was not merely a religion but a complete, separate, civilisation with its own cultural codes and morality, capable of providing a viable alternative to Western civilisation. In his view, adopting European civilisation would lead to a schizophrenic society. Thus, Turkey could only progress if its development was based on authentic Turkish-Islamic culture. Necip Fazıl and his followers emphatically looked for continuities with the Ottoman past, a period always rejected by the Kemalist elite. Necip Fazıl formulated his ideas on cultural policy in the magazines of the 1930s and 1940s. One of these (dating from 1943), already bore the name of 'The Great East' (Büyük Doğu) (Yavuz 2003: 114-6).

IBDA-C is a very radical organisation, related to some movements in the Arab world that fall under the umbrella name of *Salafiyya*, and whose goal it is to create a pure Islamic state in the image of the community of their 'pious forefathers' (*al-salaf al-sâlih*, from which the name of Salafiyya is derived) (Shinar in EI2, vol. VIII: 900b). The movement does not recognise the Turkish Republic, but it also rejects the Iranian Shiite regime. Its ideal is a federal Islamic state which, by replacing nation-states, removes differences within the Islamic world. IBDA-C had a charismatic leader in its founder, Salih İzzet Erdiş, better known under his pseudonym of Salih Mirzabeyoğlu, who has been in a Turkish prison since 1998. He is the author of many texts on theoretical and tactical issues.

IBDA-C's organisation is opaque. One branch operates through overt activities, such as holding demonstrations, publishing magazines and maintaining websites. However, there is also a covert cell-based organisation, involved in 'struggle', which boils down to attacks and hijacks. It is a horizontal organisation in which the cells are kept strictly separated and frequently operate independently. The operations these cells undertake, fit the concept of 'armed propaganda', a tactic also frequently employed by left-wing urban guerrillas in Turkey during the 1970s. It entails attacks on high-publicity targets of low military risk, such as secularist newspapers and journalists, synagogues, a prominent Jewish businessman and a Greek Orthodox Church (www.ict.org.il, 4-12-2003). It is highly probable that IBDA-C members, either with or without al-Qaeda assistance, were also behind the suicide bombings in Istanbul in November 2003.

135

2.4.4 HIZBULLAH

A younger, but significantly larger extremist Islamic organisation is *Hizbullah* (Party of God, the name refers to a quotation from the Koran). This organisation, which is unrelated to the Shiite *Hizbullah* in Lebanon, grew up in the late 1980s in Kurdish southeast of Turkey. Its main centres were the provinces of Batman and Diyarbakır, the 'capital' of the southeast. This period witnessed a rapid escalation of the war between the Turkish army and PKK guerrillas. In principle, Hizbullah was opposed to both sides in the conflict, since its ideal was the establishment of an independent Islamic state. In practice, Hizbullah's terror campaign was mainly aimed against the 'godless' PKK and against progressive Turks, and in particular against Kurdish businessmen and journalists suspected of supporting the PKK. In the early 1990s, the organisation split into two branches, both named after the bookshop where their respective supporters assembled: the *İlim* (Knowlegde) branch and the *Menzil* (Stage) branch. The violence of the 1980s was mainly committed by the İlim branch (www.terrorism.com, 3-12-2003).

By the late 1990s, there were growing rumours that Turkish security services had infiltrated the İlim faction to such a degree that it had actually
become an instrument of the Turkish state in its struggle against the PKK
(Zürcher 1995: 381-2). These rumours seemed to be confirmed when the
Turkish media, perhaps informed by rivalling intelligence services,
produced evidence indicating that the governor of Batman had been
engaged in large-scale illegal weapons smuggle. After the capture of PKK
leader Abdullah Öcalan in early 1999, which actually ushered in the end of
the war, the Turkish state no longer needed Hizbullah. The military
campaign against fundamentalism, which was been launched in February
1997, could now also be used against Hizbullah militants. Hüseyin
Velioğlu, the leader of the İlim faction, was killed in Istanbul by the security services. In a subsequent year-long campaign, another two thousand of
its members were arrested and hundreds charged. The real dimensions of
Hizbullah's gruesome legacy only emerged when the police at various sites
uncovered about seventy bodies of murdered Turkish and Kurdish business figures and intellectuals, which clearly bore signs of torture.

In 2001-2001, Hizbullah murdered several Turkish civil servants, including
the commissioner of Diyarbakır. This showed that the security services had
not fully succeeded in rounding up the organisation. Its current active
members are estimated at around one hundred.

2.4.5 THE CALIPHATE OF COLOGNE

The third known organisation with a clearly fundamentalist manifesto is
the so-called 'Caliphate State', founded by Cemalettin Kaplan. Born in 1926
in a village in the province of Erzurum, Kaplan completed his studies at a
theological college in Ankara in 1966. Until 1971, he worked as a mufti in
the service of the Directorate of Religious Affairs in Adana. In the 1970s, he
joined Necmettin Erbakan's National Vision movement. Like many Milli
Görüş supporters, he left Turkey after the military coup in September 1980
and the banning of the then Islamic National Salvation Party, establishing
himself in the German city of Cologne. He broke away from the National
Vision movement in 1983, after having become convinced that participation in the democratic political system was not compatible with Islam. In
Cologne he founded the *İsslamî Cemiyetler ve Cemaatler Birliği* (Union of
Islamic Associations and Municipalities), which at its peak attracted around
seven thousand supporters, including also Dutch Turks.

Kaplan's message was extraordinarily radical. He modelled himself on the
Ayatollah Khomeini and called on his followers to overthrow the Turkish
secular order and proclaim an Islamic state. Like Khomeini, who had sent
tapes to Iran in the 1970s, he sent cassette tapes to Turkey, earning him the

nickname *Kara Ses* (Black Voice). He saw this as a step towards establishing a worldwide Islamic state, with the Koran functioning as constitution. At the end of 1991, he even called for a *cihat* (holy war) on the Republic of Turkey.

At a conference in Cologne in April 1992, Kaplan's movement was renamed the 'Federal Islamic State of Anatolia' (*Anadolu Federal Islamî Devleti*), and in 1994 once again renamed 'Caliphate State' (*Hilafet Devleti*). Kaplan himself was appointed caliph. Not all his followers agreed to these changes. To maintain control over his movement, Kaplan transferred all its material possessions to an independent foundation in Dordrecht, the Netherlands, known as the 'Servant of Islam Foundation'.

Cemalettin Kaplan died in May 1995, whereupon his son Metin assumed the duties of caliph. Under his leadership, the movement declined. Against a rival contender for the caliphate in Berlin, who refused to recognise him, Metin pronounced a *fetva* (religious advice). When his followers responded by murdering the contender, Metin received a four-year prison sentence. After repeated requests by Turkey, the Caliphate State was finally outlawed by a German judge in 2001, on the grounds of calling for the overthrow of the constitutional order and inciting hatred. Nevertheless, the organisation's activities continue, both in Germany and abroad. The best-known propaganda organs are the magazine *Ümmet-i Muhammed* (Community of Mohammed) and the newspaper *Beklenen Asr-i Saadet* (The Expected Time of Exaltation). In the Netherlands, too, this paper has a small but loyal readership (www.im.nrw.de, 4-12-2003).

137

2.5 CHRISTIANS AND JEWS IN TURKEY

2.5.1 NON-MUSLIMS IN THE MUSLIM COMMUNITY

According to national population statistics, some 99 per cent of Turkey's population of around 70 million is Muslim, including Alevis. The various Christian groups make up about 0.3 per cent of the population and the Jewish community about 0.04 per cent. Apart from very small groups of Catholics and Protestants, Turkish Christians consist of four main groups: Greek Orthodox, Armenians, Nestorians and Syrian Orthodox. Members of the first two groups almost all live in Istanbul, whereas members of the latter two can be found both in Istanbul and the southeast of Turkey. The Jewish community is concentrated in Istanbul (Sunier 1998: 47-8, 76).

The Christian and Jewish communities in Turkey are thus many times smaller than the Islamic population groups of, for example, the Nether-lands. One could wonder, then, whether these miniscule groups deserve a place in this survey of the Turkish religious landscape. At the same time, events from a fairly recent past have shown that the position of Christians in Turkey is a politically and socially sensitive issue, capable of arousing strong emotions. Motions on the Turkish treatment of Armenian Christians have frequently been debated in the past, even within the American congress and the French parliament. Since the 1970s, Jewish organisations and prominent members of the Jewish community in Turkey have been the targets of attacks.

The Netherlands has also been confronted with the tensions and emotions sparked by the problem of 'dissident thinkers' in Turkey. About 25 years ago, Dutch newspapers were full of stories about church occupations in Twente. This was the work of Syrian Orthodox immigrants from Midyat in southeast Turkey, who were seeking political asylum in the Netherlands because they feared persecution in Turkey. These events suddenly drew attention to the fact that the small town Glanerbrug in Twente had become the religious centre of Syrian Orthodox people in Europe. And just a few years ago, the municipality of Assen in the Netherlands faced serious problems after granting permission to its Armenian community to erect an Armenian cross, which included an inscription commemorating the victims of Turkish violence. This led to fierce Turkish protests.

To understand the apparent contrast between the numerical insignificance and the charged emotions surrounding the theme of 'Christians and Jews in Turkey', a historical retrospect is needed.

2.5.2 THE 'PEOPLE OF THE BOOK'

From the start of the Arab conquests of the 7th century AD, Islamic rulers had to find a way of accommodating large groups of non-muslims. After all, the majority of the population in areas such as Syria or Egypt were Christians. The conversion to Islam of large parts of these peoples was a very gradual process.

The religious and legal basis for association with non-Muslims was provided by the concept of the 'people of the Book.' Jews and Christians were acknowledged as having received the same divine revelations as Muslims, albeit that the account of this revelation in their scriptures was corrupted, and they themselves had strayed from the true path. In Muslim eyes, both groups had a fundamentally different status from, for instance, Hindus, Buddhists, animists or fire-worshippers, who were seen as real 'heathens'. As a rule, the 'people of the Book' were offered the status of *dhimmi* (protégé). In exchange for the payment of a specific poll tax, their presence was tolerated. They maintained a large degree of autonomy in their community's internal affairs, under supervision of their own churches or rabbinical authority.

Until the middle of the 19th century, Christians and Jews in the Ottoman Empire did not enjoy the same rights as Muslims. Their second-class status was visible through building and clothing regulations, a ban on church bells and the building of new churches, etc. However, this system produced a degree of religious tolerance that most other European countries attained only after the French Revolution. For the Ottomans, establishing a workable system for associating with Christian minorities was all the more important, since their conquests on the European continent had brought large areas with Christian populations under their control. By the mid-19th century, around forty per cent of the Ottoman Empire's population was Christian. Just before the start of the First World War, their share was still around twenty per cent. The Ottoman administration displayed the same love for regulations and bureaucracy towards the dhimmis as it did towards Islam, which it tried to incorporate into its own state apparatus.

In the Ottoman Empire, the dhimmis of a specific faith were collectively referred to as *tayfa* (community) or *millet* (nation). The latter word did not carry the political baggage of its modern-day equivalent. The three millets whose existence was officially recognised by the Ottomans were the Greek Orthodox, the Armenian-Jacobite and the Jewish ones. Although in theory the term covered the entire collectivity of a specific faith, the self-government of religious minorities had in fact a local character, allowing local religious leaders to act as intermediaries between the local representatives of the Ottoman Empire on the one hand, and their own local community on the other. The authorities held religious leaders responsible for the loyalty and good behaviour of their followers (Braude and Lewis 1982; Lewis 1996: 315-8).

2.5.3 FOREIGNERS AND PROTÉGÉS

Apart from indigenous Christian populations, small groups of subjects of European states were also present in the Ottoman Empire, primarily for trading purposes. They were concentrated in the important trading centres: Istanbul, of course, but also towns like Aleppo, Salonica, Izmir, Akko and Beirut. These Europeans were not subjects of the sultan, and their stay in the Ottoman Empire was protected by a letter of safe-conduct (*aman*, literally, mercy). This was essential, since under Islamic law there formally existed a state of war between the areas under Islamic control (*dar ul-islam*, or 'house of Islam) and the areas not (yet) under Islamic control (*dar ul-harb*, or 'house of war'). In theory, these letters of safe-conduct for people originating from the 'house of war' were only valid for one year. In practice, however, Europeans often stayed within the Ottoman Empire for years on end, even for generations. The conditions under which they were allowed to reside and trade, were laid down in so-called *ahdnames* ('letters of promise'), in the West called 'capitulations' (because they were divided into chapters). The Ottoman government granted these as a favour to friendly European states (De Groot 1986: 7-9).

Apart from tax perks, the privileges extended by the sultans included a certain degree of extraterritoriality. The leaders of foreign communities – consuls or, in Istanbul, ambassadors – were empowered to conduct all those affairs which exclusively concerned the members of their own nation, both independently and according to their own, say, French, English or Dutch, laws. To maintain contact with the Ottoman authorities, these representatives of the European states employed interpreters, or *dragomans*, who nearly always belonged to one of the indigenous Christian groups. Since these were positions involving confidentiality, the Ottoman government allowed these local Christians to enjoy the protection of their European ambassador or consul, and to enjoy the status of subject of their employer's nation. Dragomans and their families received this status though a so-called 'diploma' (*berat*).

From the late 18th century onwards, the military and political position of the Ottoman Empire weakened in relation to its Christian neighbours. At the same time, trade with Europe expanded rapidly. This economic climate led to the merger of the capitulations system and the millet system. The more a great European state managed to increase its power towards the Ottoman Empire, the more valuable became its protection. For indigenous Christian traders who were or became involved in trade with Europe, especially for the Greeks, the honorary citizenship of a European power provided both security and tax advantages. Conversely, for European states these protégés were an appealing group of clients who enabled them to strengthen their power base in the Levant. Since the Ottoman authorities could charge a great deal of money for the *berats*, their issuing proved very tempting. Between 1770 and 1850, the number of Ottoman Christians and Jews in the possession of a *berat* increased explosively, from a few thousand at the most, to hundreds of thousands.

In the 19th century, the Ottoman Empire witnessed the growth of a sizeable, modern commercial and industrial sector, mainly located in the coastal areas. This sector was completely dominated by Christian, and sometimes Jewish, protégés of European powers. They formed a bourgeoisie who modelled their lifestyles on the examples of London and Paris. From the 1830s onward, however, successive Ottoman governments began reforming the state apparatus and the army, to counter Europe's growing power. Their model was that of a centralised bureaucratic state with a large army of conscripts. In the course of the 19th century, then, Ottoman society became polarised, between a growing Christian, and partly Jewish, bourgeoisie on the one hand, and a state apparatus dominated by Muslims on the other.

The Christian minorities in the Ottoman Empire of the 19th century pursued three different and completely incompatible goals. The first was equal citizenship within the Ottoman state – in the sense of obtaining the same rights as the Muslim majority. The European powers strongly urged the Turks to introduce equality of civil rights irrespective of religion, even though this sometimes flagrantly contradicted the state of affairs in their own territories. In 1856, the Ottoman government granted equal justice to all subjects. In the 1860s, the mainly younger members of the Ottoman bureaucracy tried to create a feeling of national identity in the form of Ottoman patriotism which could be shared equally by all communities, but these attempts failed. The combination of autonomy, foreign protection and growing prosperity gave Christians the opportunity to develop their own sense of community, with their own media, public spaces and associations. A variety of nationalisms developed from this, creating an increasingly powerful force.

Independence, or at least autonomy within their own national borders, was the second goal that ever more Ottoman Christians pursued increasingly energetically. During the 19th century and the beginning of the 20th century, first the Serbs and the Greeks, and subsequently the Romanians, Bulgarians, Monte-Negrians and Albanians all managed to establish sovereign independent states in what they considered to be part of their national territory. From about 1880, Armenians residing in Anatolia also started a nationalist movement. Apart from equal rights and nationalist aspirations, the third Christian goal was the preservation of the privileges and autonomy enjoyed by the *millets* under the old order. This included the right to maintain and implement ones own religious laws, the right to own education systems in one's own languages and, in general, the right to preserve ones own culture (Lewis 1996: 316-8).

2.5.4 ETHNO-RELIGIOUS CONFLICTS

Facing, what he considered, a doubtful loyalty of his Christian subjects, which had already come to light in the disastrous 1877-8 war against Russia, Sultan Abdülhamit II tried to create a more solid foundation for his regime by explicitly profiling it as Islamic. He more or less successfully appealed to the Islamic population, which by 1878 made up around eighty per cent of the population. Obviously, though, this still further alienated non-Muslim minorities from the state.

The opposition to the regime which developed towards the end of the 1890s, was actually a monstrous alliance. It was made up of, on the one hand, members of minority groups demanding decentralisation and more autonomy, and on the other of young Muslim bureaucrats and soldiers who actually tried to stop the undermining of state powers. Their opposing goals clearly emerged when in 1908-1909 a group of young bureaucrats and soldiers, the Young Turks, ended the autocratic regime of Sultan Abdül-hamit. Once the euphoria had passed, the differences between these two groups quickly flared up again.

The Balkan war of 1912-1913 eventually proved to be the breaking point. The Ottoman Empire lost almost all of its European territories. Moreover, these were territories from which a disproportionately large number of political and military leaders originated, such as Mustafa Kemal Pasja. Greece had been an opponent during the war, and many Ottoman Greeks had hoped for an Ottoman defeat. When this did indeed happen, hundreds of thousands of Muslims were expelled from the Balkan region. Subsequent reprisals by the Ottomans meant that in 1914 about 130,000 Greeks on the Anatolian west coast were expelled from the Empire.

During the First World War, there were further repercussions. As a result of the Ottoman Empire's war with England, France and Russia, these states lost the possibility to safeguard their protégés residing within the Empire. This allowed the regime under the Young Turks to take charge. Economically, this meant the logical application of a new policy, which aimed at ridding modern sectors of all quasi-monopoly positions held by minorities, and at creating a new class of Muslim entrepreneurs.

Apart from discrimination, the regime also actively engaged in deportations and persecutions. Determined to avoid in Anatolia what had happened earlier on the Balkan, the Young Turks deported almost the entire Armenian population to the Syrian desert, because some Armenian groups had chosen to side with Russia and had attacked the Ottoman army. These deportations, which took place under terrible conditions, were also used to conduct mass-scale slaughter among the Armenians. In total, probably between 600,000 and 800,000 Armenians were killed. In turn, Armenian resistance groups who accompanied the Russian army also kept their end up.

The all-encompassing dividing-line between Ottoman Muslims and Ottoman Christians remained in place after the First World War. The resistance movement created in Anatolia under the leadership of Mustafa

Kemal Pasja, opposed the division of the Ottoman Empire that was stipu-
lated by the Paris Peace Conference. As a result, it came into conflict with
Great Britain and France, even though the actual armed struggle was
conducted against the Armenians and the Greeks, who claimed large parts
of Anatolia. Both sides in the conflict acted ruthlessly against the civil
population. When Turkish nationalists won the wars against the Armenians (in 1929) and the Greeks (in 1922), all parties in the conflict recognised
that relationships between Muslims and Christians had deteriorated to
such an extent that their co-existence in one state was no longer possible.
The Greek population in the west of Anatolia fled en masse. During the
peace negotiations in Lausanne in 1923, where present-day Turkey was
mapped out, Greece and Turkey reached an agreement, under the auspices
of the League of Nations, to swap the remaining Muslims in Greece for the
remaining Greek Orthodox population in Turkey. Since these population
exchanges were enforced, the 'Greeks' of Middle Anatolia, who were
mostly Turkish-speaking, as well as the Greek community of the Black Sea
coast all left. All in all, large numbers of people were involved: in the 1922-
1924 period some 1.2 million Greeks left the country, whilst some 400,000
Muslims returned.The only non-Islamic groups of any significance which
stayed behind were those Greeks who could prove that they had lived in
Istanbul before 1912, the Armenian community of Istanbul, the Jews of
Istanbul (both Sephardic and Ashkenazic) and the Catholic and Protestant
communities, most of whom carried foreign passports. By far the largest of
these remaining groups was the Greek community of Istanbul, with more
than 100,000 members in 1924.

2.5.5 NON-MUSLIMS IN THE REPUBLIC

In articles 38-44 of the Treaty of Lausanne, non-Muslims (*gayrimüslim*)
were officially recognised as minorities and their rights in the new Republic
were laid down and declared internationally binding. They were the only
population group in Turkey who could (and still can) claim these rights.
Apart from outlawing discrimination and guaranteeing the freedom of religion, these articles also provided minorities with the right to use their own
languages and to have their own educational institutions (Parla 1985: 8-10).

The secularisation policy of the Republic, which was of course primarily
aimed at Islam, was welcomed in principle by the Christian and Jewish
minorities. The Muslim population, however, was deeply traumatized.
The Republic's nationalist regime originated from a movement that had
defended the rights of Muslims against local and foreign Christians. The
semi-colonial situation was still fresh in their memories. It had meant
that the entire modern sector of the economy was run by Christian
protégés of European states, and that Muslims working in, say, the

Ottoman Bank, could not attain positions beyond those of cleaners or doormen. Furthermore, this dependence on minorities was not just something of the (recent) past. The teaching of modern skills to ensure that Muslims could replace Christians and Jews, took over a generation. In Anatolia this meant that in many areas there was a lack of qualified engineers, waiters, managers, welders, electricians, etc. In Istanbul, where minority groups had for the most part been allowed to stay, they continued to dominate these occupations. In addition, these groups dominated the classes of the self-employed well until the 1950s. Already in the 1920s, dissatisfaction with this situation had prompted the authorities to impose discriminatory measures. When foreign enterprises, such as the railways, were taken over by the Turkish state, this change was often also used to replace as many Christian and Jewish employees as possible with Muslims (Bali 1999: 206 ff).

It should come as no surprise that such measures left a reasonable doubt among minorities about the truly neutral and secular character of the Republic. Their worst suspicions were confirmed during the Second World War. This brought large economic problems and widespread impoverishment upon neutral Turkey, for which the government party and its allies in the media blamed the Greek, Armenian and Jewish business communities. The result was the introduction in 1942 of a wealth tax (*Varlık Vergisi*), the imposition of which was left to local committees. These made sure that the tax was shifted onto minorities, who often had to pay up to ten times as much as Muslims. Moreover, they were not allowed to pay in instalments, which meant that many were forced to sell their businesses under very unfavourable conditions. Those that were unable to pay, were deported to labour camps in East Anatolia. The law was revoked in 1944, but by then it had already severely damaged minorities' trust in the Turkish state. After the war, a process of steady emigration got underway.

The Jews were the first group to emigrate en masse. It is true that Turkey had allowed many European Jews unobstructed passage to Palestine, and had also offered shelter to several tens of thousands during the Second World War. However, like other minorities, the Jews had suffered under the *Varlık Vergisi*. Moreover, the climate had worsened even before the war; soon after Hitler's rise to power in 1934, Jews in European Turkey had suffered persecutions instigated by Nazi-sympathisers (Bali 1999: 243). The creation of the state of Israel in 1948 thus prompted many Turkish Jews to leave the country. The Jewish community in Turkey shrank from approximately 80,000 after the war, to less than 50,000 in 1955. Its numbers steadily declined until the Israeli victory in the Six Day's War of 1967, when a second wave of emigrants again halved the community's numbers.

Today there are about 18,000 Jews in Turkey, the vast majority living in Istanbul. They still play a relatively important role in the business world, but do not emphasise their Jewish identity. Attacks on Jewish targets by ultra-left or fundamentalist groups (especially the assault on Istanbul's main synagogue, which has been attacked three times since 1989), have increased fears among Jews of exposing their identity. The rise of the Welfare Party in the early 1990s was also intimidating for Jews, since the party harboured a clearly recognisable anti-Semitic undercurrent, connecting anti-Israeli rhetoric with praise for Hitler and references to a Jewish conspiracy controlling US and EU policies (Erbakan 1975: 235-64; Poulton 1997: 279-81).

The only exception to this 'low profile' of the Jewish community is the resurgent interest in the Spanish-language (Ladino) culture of the Sephardic Jews, who had found refuge in Turkey at the end of the 15th century. While this culture was threatened with extinction only some ten years ago, the 1992 celebration of the 500th anniversary of Jewish immigration signalled its revival. Since it accentuates traditions of tolerance and freedom of religion in Turkey, it was also welcomed by the state. By now, Sephardic music in particular attracts a wide audience.

The Greek minority recovered after the Second World War, when relations between Greece and Turkey were warm. However, this ended abruptly after the outbreak in the mid-1950s of a crisis over the future of Cyprus. To increase diplomatic pressure upon the Greeks, the Turkish Menderes administration had demonstrations organised against the oppression of the Turkish minority on Cyprus. On 6 and 7 September 1955, these ended in an anti-Greek pogrom, in which several people died and countless houses and shops were plundered and set alight. Schools, churches and cemeteries also fell victim to popular anger. At that point, the Greeks lost their faith in the Republic for good, and they have been emigrating ever since. Istanbul's Greek community of 100,000 to 150,000 people in 1923, has now shrunk to three or four thousand people.

Ironically, of all the religious minorities in today's Turkey, the Armenians are both the largest in number and the ones to have suffered most in the past. Like the Greek Orthodox community, they suffered from (sometimes state-fuelled) resentment from the Muslim population. In the 1970s and 1980s, they sometimes became the victims of reprisals for the worldwide campaign of attacks on Turkish targets committed by the Armenian Secret Army for the Liberation of Armenia (ASALA). Still, Istanbul's Armenian community today consists of 30,000 to 35,000 people.

The small Christian communities in the southeast, the Nestorians and Syrian Orthodox, have had a very tough time since the 1970s, caught between the Turkish army, radical Muslims of Hizbullah and Kurdish guerrillas. Economically, matters did not improve in what was already the poorest region of Turkey. Almost all of these communities have therefore left for the relative safety of Istanbul or have emigrated to Europe. The Syrian community in Twente, the Netherlands, serves as an example (Poulton 1997: 272-8).

2.5.6   IS A TURK A MUSLIM?

The above description of the fate of non-Islamic minorities clearly raises the question as to what extent Christians and Jews are really seen as fully-fledged Turkish citizens, and to what extent they see themselves as such.

Formally, the situation is crystal clear. The Turkish state and Turkish legislation do not discriminate on the basis of religion. Turkish nationality is essentially still defined on the basis of Atatürk's principles of the 1930s: "Every person within the Republic of Turkey, irrespective of his religion, is a Turk if he speaks Turkish, grows up in the Turkish culture, and embraces the Turkish ideal" (Zürcher in Georgeon (ed.) 2000: 60). At the same time, Turkey's late 19th and early 20th century history has produced a certain 'siege mentality'; a notion that foreign powers are intent on weakening or even splitting up the country, by using fifth columns. People quickly feel threatened, and the war against the PKK during the last two decades has strengthened this feeling. There is always a tendency to see minorities as accomplices of foreign enemies.

In addition, it has not always been easy for members of minority groups to consider themselves as fully-fledged Turkish citizens. The embrace of Sunni Islam by the nationalist state ideology which began in 1980, has severely damaged their integration. By far the larger majority of Christians and Jews have voted with their feet and have emigrated. This has further weakened the position of those staying behind.

3 TURKISH ISLAM AND THE EU: A CLASH OF CIVILISATIONS?

In the previous part of this survey, we have made acquaintance with several important characteristics of Turkish Islam, and also with the large variety of Turkey's religious landscape. In this chapter, we wish to answer the question to what extent the fact that Turkey is an Islamic country will turn out to be an insurmountable impediment to its membership of the EU. In other words: does Islam block Turkey's accession to the EU? The discussion takes place against the wider backdrop of yet another debate, i.e. on the place in this landscape of Samuel Huntington's notion of the 'clash of civilisations'. Implicitly, therefore, this leads us to an assessment of the validity of his paradigm, which has been widely used since its launch in 1993, especially in politics and journalism.

3.1 MODERN VERSUS WESTERN

Characteristic of Huntington's approach (apart from his dividing of the world into 'civilisations'), is his distinction between the West and modernity, or put differently: between Westernisation and modernisation. Since the 18th century, all modernisation processes (which include elements such as industrialisation, urbanisation, literacy, education, prosperity, labour specialisation and social mobilisation), have their roots in European civilisation, which was the first to modernise. In principle, modernisation is a revolutionary process that is universal. Nations such as Japan and China prove that countries from different civilisations can also undergo a successful modernisation process. According to Huntington, this does not mean that Western culture will therefore also becomes a universal culture. He emphatically discards the notion that 'modern' and 'Western' are identical. With the 'clash of civilisations' he no longer believes (as he once did) that advancing modernisation will allow values that are characteristic of Western civilisation to become universal. His explanation for this is that Western civilisation was formed in the era preceding the start of the process of modernisation of the 17th and 18th centuries. The West was already the West before it became modern. Other areas of the world take part in this modernisation process, without possessing the cultural legacy of the premodern West (Huntington 2002: 68-72).

According to Huntington, the historical elements which combine to give Western civilisation its characteristic properties, are the legacy of classical antiquity, Catholicism and Protestantism, the wealth of languages, the separation of spiritual and worldly powers, the development of law, social plurality (a class-based society), representative bodies and individualism.

147

All these ingredients are connected: social plurality has stimulated the rise of representative bodies, while many of these characteristics have ultimately contributed to the importance that the West attaches to the individual (Huntington 2002: 68-72).

Unlike the process of modernisation, Western civilisation thus has clear borders, i.e. the borders defining the area within which the above-mentioned historical factors have operated. As Huntington puts it: "Europe ends where Western Christianity ends and Islam and Orthodox begin" (2002: 158). It is this reasoning which found its political translation in statements of people like Bolkestein, Giscard d'Estaing, Kohl and Martens, who have all argued that Turkey should not accede to the EU, because it is not a part of Western nor of European civilisation.

There is a problem with the notion that Europe is an historically-grown civilisation. Therefore, there is also a problem with the political conclusion that the EU's external borders should not move beyond the borders of European civilisation. To start with, neither the current nor the candidate EU member states fulfil Huntington's criteria. After all, the influence of Catholicism and Protestantism remains negligible in Greece. And what influence did classical civilisation have on (pre-modern) Finland? At the same time, countries which Huntington has slotted into the Islamic bloc, such as Turkey and Syria, did share in classical culture, among other things. That these areas later came under Arab or Turkish administration does not alter this, unless one would assert – historically incorrectly – that their original inhabitants departed en masse after the Arab and Turkish conquests.

Worse still is the fact that Huntington applies criteria which display his ignorance of other civilisations, and of Islam in particular (which Huntington sees as 'the West's' main opponent). It is an affront to assert that the classical legacy played a lesser role in the Islamic world than in the Western world, when that legacy was actually passed on to medieval Europe by Arab translations of, and annotations to the classics. The diversity of languages, which is supposed to be an exclusive characteristic of Europe, is not exactly a convincing argument for those studying the Caucasus or Indonesia. The statement that in other civilisations, including in Islam, law was less of a deciding factor in shaping philosophy and behaviour is, frankly, bizarre to anyone who is a little familiar with Islamic societies' fixation with the rules of the holy law. It is belied by the crucial role across the entire Islamic world, and for over a thousand years, of the institute of legal adviser, the mufti.

Naturally, this is all general criticism of Huntington's empirical basis and of his theoretical assumptions. On closer examination, the borders between civilisations turned out to be grey and porous. But can something be said on Turkey's specific position in the light of the 'clash of civilisations'?

3.2   THE POSITION OF TURKEY

Huntington ranks Turkey among the 'torn countries'. These are countries where the elite aspires to cross from one civilisation to another. In his view, this will only succeed if three conditions are fulfilled: the elite must be enthusiastic, the population must be willing to accept the cross-over and the 'receiving civilisation' must be prepared to accept the country. Huntington observes that such a reshaping of identity is a long, step-by-step and painful process, which has never succeeded so far (Huntington 2002: 139). He does suggest, though, that Islam's wide area means there are many distinct cultures or subcivilisations within Islam, including Arab, Turkish, Persian and Malay civilisations (Huntington 2002: 44-5). In other words, due to certain factors, variants emerge within a so-called 'major civilisation'.

149

In section 2.1.2, we typified the Republic of Turkey's Ottoman-Islamic inheritance as a tradition which, in turn, draws from two rather different and, in part, even conflicting sources. Firstly, the Islamic roots of society and, secondly, the Turkish tradition of state formation and state constitution which had taken shape in Central Asia by the 6th century and in the Middle East by the 10th century. In addition, in the border regions between the Middle East and Central Asia, the military and political traditions developed by the Turks blended with the ancient Persian monarchical tradition, which strongly emphasised the independent authority of the sovereign.

We subsequently stressed that the Ottomans succeeded in uniting the Islamic and the Turkish-Persian traditions into a single administrative system. Officially, the Ottoman Empire was an Islamic state formally based on the şeriat, the holy law. In practice, sultans could proclaim complex regulations, known as kanun, for administering the affairs of a province, of a department, or of the monarchy and the central government itself. A kanun could in no way nullify or abolish the şeriat, but it could supplement and modernise this by using local customs and by-laws of the rulers (Lewis 1996: 223-4).

One could say that even before the period of modernisation, Ottoman legacy was characterised by a combination of different systems and traditions in various areas, adapted to the practical circumstances confronting the Ottomans. In Huntington's terminology, this would mean that there would be no 'clash of civilisations', but rather a pragmatic 'composition of civilisations' within the political realm of the Ottoman Empire. The Ottoman attitudes toward heterodox minorities, and also their treatment of Christians and Jews, displayed the same pragmatic mentality.

Cemal Kafadar (1995) had this to say about the issue of Ottoman identity:

"The Ottoman state/identity was not a lid that closed upon already formed national identities (of Arabs, Bulgarians, Turks, etc.) only to be toppled after a few centuries when those identities reasserted themselves. Some of these identities were formed to some extent, but they were reshaped (some might say, de-formed) under the aegis of, through the structures of, in response or reaction to, the Ottoman Empire. This is not a question of Ottoman influence but of a long and formative historical experience that shaped various communities and peoples under Ottoman rule through their interaction with each other as well as with peoples and ideas from neighbouring civilizations. So the establishment of Ottoman rule in southwestern Asia and southeastern Europe, even if one sees it in black-and-white terms – namely, as either a yoke or a blessing – did mean much more than a lapse in what would otherwise have been the natural flow of the history of a given set of nations. Ottoman rule is part of the history of various communities, some of whom were able (and some unable) to shape and imagine themselves into a nation in the modern era thanks to a 'historical consciousness' of their own (real or imagined) pre-Ottoman identity on the one hand and to the long and formative historical experience mentioned above on the other. (…) Historians tend to overlook the fact that (America is not the only case where) one is not necessarily born into a people; one may also become of a people, within a socially constructed dialectic of inclusions and exclusions" (Kafadar 1995: 22-7).

Further on, he presents us with one of those hot potatoes which have produced different interpretations of Ottoman state building.

"(…) The creation of the Ottoman administrative apparatus has been particularly controversial, with some historians arguing that it was all based on Byzantine models and others that the Ottomans could find all they needed in the Turko-Muslim heritage. In terms of broader cultural exchange or 'lifestyles' too, various sides of nationalist polemics have tended to see the influence of their side in, say, shared musical or culinary practices. The problem with both sides of this debate stems partly from their adherence to a static notion of cultural 'goods', whether one conceives of them in the realm of state building or cooking. In other words, 'influence' is understood as a creative party giving one of its own 'goods' to an imitating, uncreative other – a notion that needs to be recast now that historians realize influence is not possible without interaction, without a choice by the allegedly passive receiver. And even then, common cultural traits are not necessarily reducible to influence" (Kafadar 1995: 24).

Kafadar's observations, though mainly concerned with the creation of the Ottoman Empire in Anatolia, are just as applicable to the five centuries of Ottoman presence in southeastern Europe. Among the opponents of Turkey's EU accession, it has become customary to discount Ottoman presence as foreign oppression, a typical example of non-European yoke under which Greeks, Bulgarians, Serbs, Hungarians, Romanians and Albanians suffered for hundreds of years. This idea, which is equally wrong, has its roots both in the centuries-old European fear of 'the Turk' (the so-called *Turca Terribilis* (De Groot 1986: 1), the only strong opponent of the European states during the early modern period), and in the nationalist rewriting of Balkan history since the 19th century. Ottoman history shares in the cultural heritage of that region, just as Ottoman culture itself was, in turn, also shaped by that region's influences.

With this we return to Huntington's thesis that Turkey is a 'torn country', willing to cross from one civilisation to another, from Islamic to Western civilisation. Following his own notion of the three pre-conditions for success, the bottleneck would lie in the reluctance on the part of the receiving civilisation (in this case, the EU) to accept Turkey. This would mean that the West is actually responsible for Turkey's 'tornness', and not the Turkish elite or the Turkish people who, according to successive 'Eurobarometer' opinion polls, are overwhelmingly (seventy per cent or more) in favour of joining the Union.

If Huntington's civilisation blocs exist, this means that Muslim Turkey is not only prepared knowingly to cross from 'the house of Islam' to the Western 'house of war', but is even willing to do its utmost to achieve this. This is not at all logical. Might it not simply be that secular Turkey has acted rationally and pragmatically, in line with historical, social and economic developments under the Ottoman Empire and the Republic? Should not we also say that the West, the EU in this case, has indeed created the Copenhagen criteria as a 'secular yardstick' to test the progress of candidate members, but that the many statements on the clash of civilisations indicate that Islam is seen as the real the problem? In short, is it not true that the West, with its so-called crucial legacy of the 'separation of powers', is really the party failing to separate politics from religion?

3.3   VALUES AS CULTURAL LEGACY

Hopefully, it is clear from the above how very hard it really is to think in terms of separate civilisations, and thus also in terms of a 'European civilisation'. It is a paradigm with large practical consequences, because Huntington considers the value systems of humanism, individualism, democracy and human rights as historical acquisitions of the 'Western world',

151

and not as an inseparable part of the modernisation process. This is why he thinks they are culturally-linked, and not universal. Western values should be defended forcefully and self-confidently (which is why Huntington rejects the concept of multiculturalism), but it is doubtful whether other great civilising blocs, such as China or 'Islam', will be open to developing a similar kind of modernity, based on the same underlying values. In this view then, Islam, in particular, is seen as an ideological system that ultimately does not tolerate democratic and humanist values (a conclusion drawn earlier by fundamentalists such as Cemalettin Kaplan, the caliph of Cologne).

From Turkey's perspective, this approach can be criticised in one general and one specific way. Firstly, the fact that a philosophical system is rooted in an historically-grown civilisation of one region, does not prevent that system from being adopted by another civilisation, or even from becoming universal. If that were untrue, then modern mathematics, for example, would not exist. More specifically, one can say that precisely in the case of the Ottoman Empire and Turkey, the modernisation process of the last century and a half was paralleled by the adoption and gradual internalisation of a system of values that has its origins in Renaissance, Humanism and Enlightenment. Already in 1839, liberal principles such as the inviolability of the individual and his possessions, were officially proclaimed by the sultan. Equality in the eyes of the law for all Ottoman citizens was official policy by 1856. A constitution was drawn up in 1876, a mere 28 years after the reform of the Dutch constitution by Thorbecke, who turned the Netherlands into a parliamentary democracy. The development of a democratic constitutional state in Turkey has been a long and arduous process with many setbacks, but it is nonsense to claim that 'Western' values of democracy and human rights are essentially foreign to Turkey.

3.4   TURKISH ISLAM, DEMOCRACY AND HUMAN RIGHTS

The question of whether Islam, democracy and human rights can be combined, has important practical consequences for Turkey, an Islamic country aspiring EU membership. Indeed, the EU's political leaders have defined the Union as a community of values. The values upon which the community is based, are reflected and formalised in the Copenhagen criteria of 1993, which are applied to judge the candidacy of potential member states. Their core elements are democracy and human rights, but neither concept is unambiguously described or defined in EU documentation. As far as the criterion of 'democracy' is concerned, this implies that the Union does not apply an absolute standard for democratic rule. Most definitions cover multiple manifestations. Hence, the Union does not restrict itself to one model, and the so-called annual Regular Reports employ an opera-

tional definition for monitoring purposes. EU views on the essential characteristics of an acceptable democratic system can therefore only be
deduced rather implicitly, from these monitoring reports. Given the large
variety of democratic systems across Europe, it comes as no surprise that
these reports are highly subjective on this issue. There is no such thing as a
standard 'European democracy'. This becomes apparent with a closer
examination of the actual practices within the different member states. In
the eyes of its citizens, the Netherlands is a democracy, yet several
elements in the Dutch governance system (the monarchy, appointed rather
than elected mayors, provincial commissioners and dike wardens) are, in
the eyes of, say, Americans or French, eccentric and not in the least democratic. The fact that the Dutch judiciary lacks a constitutional court, is met
with amazement in many countries. Conversely, the French phenomenon
of a parliamentary representative who is also mayor of a large city, is difficult to reconcile with Dutch conceptions of proper public administration.
The same holds for the British monarchy's position as the head of the
church, which many other Europeans view as difficult to reconcile with
the principles of secularism. The fact that the Federal Republic of Germany
collects taxes on behalf of the churches, is very suspect in the eyes of Turkish secularists.

153

Even within Europe, there is clearly no yardstick available for measuring
the central criteria of Copenhagen. We can, at most, start from a number of
minimum conditions which a system must fulfil to qualify as democratic –
conditions such as free and fair elections, peaceful transfer of power, separation of powers and the right of the parliamentary majority to form a
government. Where reports by the European Parliament provide much
more detailed information on the requirements for democracy, they find
themselves on thin ice.

The same, however, cannot be said of human rights. The definition of
human rights in the Regular Reports is based on the European Convention
on Human Rights (ECRM), laid down in Rome in 1950, and is also related
to the United Nations' Universal Declaration of Human Rights (1948),
which in turn builds on the French *Déclaration des droits de l'homme et du
citoyen* of 1789, the American Constitution of 1787 and the British Bill of
Rights of 1689.

Is Islam, as it is practiced in Turkey, in conflict with these basic principles?
To begin with, it is of course undeniable that any belief system that claims
to represent a divine and therefore absolute truth, and to express this in a
set of rules of life, inevitably runs into some form of conflict with the
pluriformity that is inherent in democratic society. The three great religions of revelation, Judaism, Christianity and Islam, are potentially the

most difficult to reconcile with democratic pluriformity, due to the central role they attribute to their respective holy books, in which revealed truth actually manifests itself. At the same time, we may conclude from the historical record of the last two hundred years, that movements which claim to be inspired by revelation, are indeed capable of playing an active and constructive role within a democratic system. In Christianity, this is demonstrated on a daily basis by the Christian democratic parties in Europe, whilst in Judaism it is evident from the roles that religious Jews have played in European and American politics, and from the history of the state of Israel. Whatever objections one might have against Israel's occupation policy, it is still undeniably a democracy.

Within the Christian and Jewish world, there are of course minorities who function within the democratic system, but who are so focused on their own revelation and divine law that their ideological principles, and sometimes also their actual practices, are in conflict with democratic pluralism and human rights. An example is the *Staatkundig Gereformeerde Partij* in the Netherlands, which de facto favours a theocracy and tramples on the constitutionally entrenched principle of equal rights for women. Other examples are the radical religious parties that emerged from the *Aguddat Israel* in Israel. Such movements, despite their dubious constitutional legitimacy, are generally tolerated as long as, in practice, they accept the rules of the democratic game. A greater problem is presented by those groups that base themselves on an interpretation of the revelation so radical and exclusive that they shun participation in the democratic system. Examples of these are the radical sects in the United States who reject the federal authority and the Jewish groups in Jerusalem who do not recognize the state of Israel. These fringe phenomena, however, have no bearing upon the fact that the vast majority of believers have found their place inside the democratic and largely secular system.

On the face of it, things are very different when it comes to Islam. It is undeniably true that the Islamic world, from Morocco to Indonesia, has a democratic deficit. In the post-colonial era, democratic political movements with an Islamic character had difficulties in developing, and since the 1970s it has mainly been radical extra-parliamentary groups who have become mouthpieces of social agitation against impoverishment, corruption and foreign policy failures. This picture seems to confirm Huntington's thesis that Islam and democracy are incompatible. But if that were the case, we would have to ignore the fact that the causes of this democratic deficit are not, as a matter of course, inherent in Islam. The military elites in North Africa and the Middle East, for example, who took power once the colonial powers had left after the Second World War, refused to involve local political and social forces into their administrations. Instead, they looked to Washington or Moscow for support. Thus, by suppressing local political activity, the opposition was wiped out, leaving a vacuum for fundamentalism to fill. According to Jansen (1998), Islamic fundamentalism can be understood as an attempt to reverse this exclusion from political and public life. He points out that, "Extreme-nationalist leaders like Qaddafi in Libya and Saddam Hussein in Iraq are [and were] dangerous, perhaps, but they are not fundamentalist" (Jansen 1998: 24). In other words, the lack of democracy in many Islamic states has more to do with the authoritarian nature of these regimes. For opportunistic reasons, they may well appeal to existing Islamic sentiments, but they are generally not fundamentalist or strongly Islamic themselves. It would therefore be wrong to conclude from the situation under such regimes that Islam excludes democracy. It would be more accurate to draw the reverse conclusion, i.e. that a lack of democracy excludes pluriformity in the religious landscape.

As yet, Turkey is the exception in the Islamic world. For over half a century, its overwhelmingly Muslim population has enjoyed a pluriform democratic system. During that period, the military have openly intervened in the political system four times, but there have also been fifteen general elections, twelve of which were truly free and fair. The country has a vocal middle class and a varied media landscape. Is Turkey then the one case which proves that Islam and democracy are indeed compatible? Or is it a front-line state in the clash between the West and Islam, in which the forces of democracy and Islam keep each other in a shaky balance? In other words, are we talking about synthesis or deadlock? As discussed extensively in section 2.1, many Kemalist secularists in Turkey perceive the latter to be the case.

Kemalists see themselves as the shock troops of secularism and 'Western' values, who are responsible for controlling the rising tide of Islam. Paradoxically, they are often prepared to make concessions on issues of democracy and human rights, to avoid the greater evil of an undemocratic social order based on religious law. Kemalists thus fail to appreciate both a set of basic characteristics of Turkish Islam, and the degree to which the secularisation process has taken root over the last 150 years. In section 2.1, we showed how Turkish-Islamic empires incorporated religious authorities into their administrative systems, thus creating a *modus vivendi* in which state (*devlet*) and religion (*din*) developed a complex relationship of mutual dependence. We have also seen how this system was refined and perfected over 600 years of Ottoman rule. Turkish ulema (Islamic religious scholars), in particular those in the higher ranks, were therefore always forced to anticipate the changing political and social circumstances facing government policies, and to find solutions which at least did not contradict

Islamic law. It is plausible that this has developed into a habit of flexibility and openness among professional practitioners of Turkish Islam – a thesis already advanced in the 1950s by Islam scholar Cantwell-Smith.

From the 1830s onwards, the symbiotic relationship between the state and Ottoman religious scholars changed as a result of a gradual but ultimately profound secularisation process. It met hardly any resistance on the part of the higher-ranking ulema. On the contrary, they sanctioned this reform process, and notable reformers, such as Ahmed Cevdet Pasja, who designed the Ottoman civil code, themselves had background as religious scholars.

This tradition was continued in the Republic. The first generations of religious scholars, now united under the banner of the Directorate of Religious Affairs, or Diyanet, supported the religious policies of the Kemalists. These aimed at driving back Islam's public role as much as possible, and rendering faith an issue of personal conviction and morality. While the postwar period produced a far more tolerant attitude towards public manifestations of religion, this did not undermine the secular order nor the secular legal system. Nor did it change the main message of state-Islam, as preached by the Diyanet. To see what this message currently is, we can take a look at one of the Diyanet's most widespread publications, the *Cep İslmihali* (pocket catechism).

3.5   THE POSITION OF OFFICIAL ISLAM

What follows is based on the Cep İslmihali of 2000. This pocket catechism consists of three chapters. The first deals with Islamic doctrine and the second with the code of conduct. The third and, for our purposes most interesting chapter is titled *İsslam'da Ahlâk* ('Islam and Ethics'). It is subdivided into five parts: the obligations of the faithful towards, respectively, God and his prophet, himself, his relatives and neighbours, his country, and humanity (Soymen 2000: 95-123). To assess to what degree this preaching of official Turkish Islam is in line with Western concepts of democracy and human rights, these last three parts are of special relevance. In Islamic ethics on relatives and neighbours, marriage and family occupy a central position. These 'institutions' are defined in traditional terms. Marriage is recommended. Those who do not marry, despite being able to, neglect their duties. A man must teach and honour his wife and treat her gently and with respect, but he is still in charge: "At home the man is the head of the family" (Soymen 2000: 108-10). The phrase about the man as head of the family has been removed from Turkey's new civil code of 2001 and replaced by the statement that husband and wife together head the family (Cumhuriyet, 22-6-2001). At the time of writing, it is still unclear to what extent this new statement is also reflected in Diyanet publications.

The chapter on the obligations towards one's country and nation strongly stress the state-allied character of official Turkish Islam. That it is clearly still dominated by the thinking of the Turkish-Islamist Synthesis (see sect. 2.1.6), is evident from statements such as: "The Islamic Turkish nation is one of the oldest, most famous, honourable and exalted nations in the history of mankind. Turkish history is full of sublime heroic deeds, which are rooted in faith." And: "Patriotism is derived from faith" (Soymen 2000: 115-17). Patriotism and national pride are not merely abstract concepts. They are translated into obedience: "Bowing before the laws and regulations of the government is a duty. Our book, the Noble Koran, orders it thus." The catechism specifies this still further in its references to the obligation to pay taxes and serve in the army: "National service ... is prescribed by the faith." National service is also appealing from a religious point of view, since: "In our faith, the position of a soldier is highly exalted. If a soldier dies, he achieves martyrdom. In the hereafter, the degree of martyrdom directly follows that of prophethood." And: "Evading national service under a pretext, or deserting the army constitutes treason, a foul act and a great sin" (Soymen 2000: 115-17).

In the chapter on the obligations towards humanity, by contrast, we find a discourse that closely fits current European notions of human rights, which are rooted in liberalism. It emphasises that God created man free, and that man is free insofar as he does not endanger the freedom of others. Islam is clearly presented as a religion more outspoken in its teachings of the natural rights of man that any other community, philosophy or science. The natural rights to which man can lay claim, are defined as: "The right to life (...), the right to freedom (...), the right to [freedom of] thought (...), and the right to ownership" (Soymen 2000: 119-20).

Summing up, the dominant current within Turkish Sunni Islam, the Diyanet's state-allied Islam, reproduces an Islam that can be characterised as adopting a middle course. Personal faith and individual morality are linked to fairly traditional social values, emphasising solidarity and hierar-chy. In this respect, the message of official Islam resembles that of Chris-tian democracy in Europe – the family as the cornerstone of society and respect for (traditional) standards and values. Ties to politics are out of the question, but religion is mobilised to promote loyalty to the state. Thus, to suggest that the Islam of the Diyanet is a liberal Islam, as is often done, is rather far-fetched. In line with Ottoman-Turkish tradition, the Directorate of Religious Affairs exudes realism and flexibility, but certainly not renewal. Daring theological interpretations are hard to find. Turkey does have its Islamic reformers, people who apply concepts from modern (Western) philosophy and sociology to arrive at a new understanding of religion, but they move outside the circles of the Diyanet and state-Islam. Among them are liberal theologian Mehmet Aydın, or publicists such as Ali Bulaç and Abdürrahman Dilipak, who call themselves 'Muslim intellectuals'.

In debates on Turkish EU membership, the existence of the Directorate of Religious Affairs and the de facto state control of (Sunni) Islam that this implies, is often presented as problematic. After all, this situation seems be completely at odds with accepted European views on the separation of church and state. However, by looking at the Diyanet's position from this angle, we tend to forget that in the Islamic world there are no institutions such as churches. As we have seen in chapter 2, protecting the faith has largely been a state concern throughout the history of the Islamic world. There is thus no body to which the state could transfer these duties. Calls for the state's withdrawal from the religious domain, are therefore hardly realistic.

However, if Turkey aspires participation in a European community of values, the Diyanet's message must be in line with those values. This means it should pay less attention to the importance of the state, and more to the role of the individual. Such a reorientation may well be possible precisely because there is this connection between religious establishment and state. This would allow the (democratising) state to insist on presenting different, more liberal interpretations of the faith. Besides, the Alevi population groups in Turkey are more than justified to claim their fair share of religious care (paid from general tax revenues).

3.6 THE VOICE OF THE OPPOSITION

Since all official authorities of Islam are incorporated in the state apparatus, irrespective of their rank, it is quite logical that occasional resistance to the secularisation policies of the late Ottoman Empire and the Republic came from the leaders of the mystical brotherhoods, who were much less caught up in the state's web (see sect. 2.2). This was indeed the case during the uprisings of 1909 and 1925, as well as the more local incidents during the 1920s and 1930s. For this reason, also, the Kemalist Republic banned the orders, and the Kemalist elite still nourishes a distrust of the brotherhoods. At the same time, though, neither the political parties which emanated from the Nakşibendi brotherhood, nor the Nurcu movement and its branches actually risked violating the secular order. The National Order Party, the National Salvation Party, the Welfare party, the Virtue Party, and the Felicity Party have all tried to gain influence through the ballot box, via normal local and national elections. While their election programmes and campaign propaganda contain many references to Islamic and traditional standards and values, explicit reference to a reintroduction of Islamic law are nowhere to be found. That may well be for tactical reasons (since this would constitute a punishable offence in Turkey), but the fact remains that in those places where the Welfare Party actually obtained power over a longer period, such as in Istanbul and Ankara after 1994, there were very few signs of actual Islamisation policies.

However, there are many signs that the 'Islamic' opposition also employs concepts such as democracy and human rights as its frame of reference, precisely because they can be used as defence mechanisms in large conflicts with the secular state apparatus. The countless female supporters of the Welfare Party who engaged in protests against the ban on headscarves in Turkish higher education, used the argument that their human rights were being violated. They demanded recognition of their rights to display their religious persuasion and accused the authorities of discrimination. In short, their arguments were not very different from those employed by Islamic women in the French debate on headscarves.

Erbakan's political movement has appeared under so many different banners because it has been banned time and again. In 1998, the Welfare Party obtained the support of around one-fifth of the Turkish electorate, was subsequently banned and its leader, Erbakan, banished from politics. However, Erbakan did not react by calling on his supporters to start a revolution and spill blood in the streets in the name of God. He took the case to the European Court (which, incidentally, decided against him), while his supporters established a new party that conformed to the Turkish law on political parties.

159

Apart from using the ballot box, Islamic movements also use other ways to gain influence. One way is by appointing their supporters to strategic positions in the state apparatus (the so-called *kadrolaşma*, of which secular Turkish parties are also guilty). Another is by educating and indoctrinating new generations of mostly underprivileged youngsters, who subsequently enter the state apparatus at the lowest rung, to become champions of Islamic standards and values. In Kemalist and European eyes, both ways are menacing, but it is difficult to maintain that they are undemocratic or in violation of human rights. In the United States, the world's democratic superpower, it is the order of the day in politics. One only has to think of the appointments to the American Supreme Court or the activities of the Christian Coalition.

To know more about the ideological principles of the most important Turkish Islamic movement, we can use Necmettin Erbakan's 1975 publication,

Milli Görüş (National Vision), as a starting point. 'National Vision' is the name of the ideological movement which has produced all of Erbakan's parties, from the National Order Party to the Felicity Party, and which also includes a broad network of mosques and associations in the Netherlands and Germany.

In his book, Erbakan emphasises that this movement is loyal to all the rights and freedoms described in the constitution. He specifically mentions the inviolability of possessions and the home, the equality of all persons before the law, and the right to trade, travel, exchange information, assemble and demonstrate (Erbakan 1975: 31-3). Like the Diyanet's catechism, its sections on the position of women emphasise their role as wives and mothers. Working women must be given the opportunity to fulfil their maternal obligations. At the same time, the movement defends the principle of equal access to education for men and women (Erbakan 1975: 38-9). National Vision pays a lot of attention to the issue of secularism. It argues that secularism in the true sense of the word (*laiklik*, from the French laïcité) allows everyone the freedom of thought, conscience, and religious practice. This is why it qualifies the Turkish system as artificial secularism, and as a system enabling non-religious people to deny religious people their human rights. Erbakan insists on dropping article 163 of the penal code, which states that political use of religion is a punishable offence. Instead, he wants a 'Law for the Protection of Human Rights' (Erbakan 1975: 51-6).

Erbakan is notably sharp in his judgement on the European Community (and later the Union), which he portrays as a neo-imperialist conspiracy by Jews and/or the Catholic Church (Erbakan 1975: 235-264). Forced by the circumstances, and especially by bearing responsibilities of government, he and his party subsequently toned down their judgement, but Milli Görüş has always remained ambivalent in its views on Europe.

In this respect, the AK Party's attitude is essentially different. In domestic policy, since 2001 the leaders of the AK Party have moved from a strongly religiously-coloured conservatism to a much more hybrid form of ethical conservatism, nationalism, free-market thinking and technologically modernisation. Moreover, their foreign policy orientation has also changed quite fundamentally. The AK Party now embraces Europe to guarantee that its strategy of bottom-up modernisation will be given a chance in confrontations with the highly restrictive and authoritarian modernisation school of the Kemalist state elite. To obtain a fuller picture of the AK Party's ideas, it is useful to look at the *AK Parti Seçim Beyannamesi*, its election manifesto, as well as its 2003 party programme, entitled: *Herşey Türkiye İçin* ('Everything for Turkey').

This first document stresses the belief in 'true' democracy, with an equal right to representation for everyone: "Our party, which sees differences of faith and culture as enriching the country, believes that people of different languages, religions, races and social status must be able to express themselves freely and participate in politics, relying on equal protection by the law" (AK Parti 2003: 7). And later: "The AK Party, which sees political parties as essential elements of the democratic system, is against the closing down of political parties which operate within the framework of the constitutional state" (AK Parti 2003: 7).

The programme further emphasises that while the AK Party strongly adheres to conservative standards and values, it also stands by a process of modernisation and further economic liberalisation, thus allowing the state to abandon its authoritarian top-down bureaucratic approach and enabling it to serve society. On the subject of accession to the EU, it says: "Our party considers complete membership of the EU as a natural consequence of the modernisation process" (AK Parti 2003: 8). In the document, the AK Party squarely supports full membership, as well as the Union's economic and political criteria. It believes that this will enhance the modernisation process, allowing society and state jointly to enhance their national and international position. Thus, these criteria are not presented as measures imposed from above to obtain an entry ticket, but rather as objective criteria that are indispensable to Turkey's domestic progress and international position. In this way, domestic opponents of EU membership are implicitly branded as opponents of their country's progress. In this line of reasoning, an ultra-nationalist is portrayed as someone who will actually damage the national interest.

161

A separate chapter deals with international agreements on fundamental human rights and freedoms. The AK Party fully endorses such agreements, also partially against the background of Turkish national interests in the global arena. It declares itself willing to do everything in its power to fulfil its international obligations agreements in general, and the requirements of the Copenhagen criteria in particular. These are said to go beyond mere legislative changes: "The respect for fundamental freedoms and rights involves more than laying down guarantees in laws and in the constitution. Additional efforts must be made to implement these changes, thus firmly ensuring their anchoring into our political culture" (AK Parti 2003: 12).

Equal rights for women are important to the AK Party. At the end of its programme, these are addressed in a separate section entitled *Kadın Sorunları* ('Problems of Women'). This states that while women and men share the same burdens of life, in practice women do not have the equal status to which they are entitled. Their main problems are said to be "economic problems, no or only low levels of education, (financial) worries about the future, domestic violence and lack of social security" (AK Parti 2003: 76), depending also on whether they live in urban or rural regions. It subsequently states, "Our party attaches importance to eliminating problems for women, since these [problems] hinder a sound upbringing of offspring and the pursuit of happiness within the family" (AK Parti 2003: 76). This is then followed by a list of measures needed to eliminate any forms of inequality or discrimination. Strikingly, it also mentions the following: "In regions where suicide amongst women and the murder of women on ethical grounds and honour killings are common, preventive and educational measures must be taken, which are directed at women and their families" (AK Parti 2003: 76). In this way, the AK Party argues that the unequal position of women and serious matters such as honour killings, have nothing to do with its interpretation of Islam, and that both practices are unacceptable.

This may well raise the following question: do we ascribe this apparent moderation of this Islamic 'opposition' to political opportunism, or to prudence? In other words, if the pressure imposed by the state and especially by the military would actually diminish, would these Islamists then also pursue a different and much more radical Islamisation of society? In a democratic political context such as that of Turkey, where votes count, this obviously leads to another question: could such a radical programme succeed in obtaining support among the people?

3.7 IS THERE A BREEDING GROUND FOR FUNDAMENTALISM?

The term 'Islamic fundamentalism' was defined earlier in this study (sect. 2.4) as a desire completely to rearrange society according to Islamic laws, sometimes also by using (political) violence. One way of gaining insight into this 'desire' is by investigating to what extent Turkish Muslims identify with such fundamentalist concepts. At the same time, it is also important to gauge the opinion of the Turkish Islamic population on 'dissident' thinkers. After all, an Islamic fundamentalist sees 'the West', its system and its philosophy as hostile to Islam.

The data presented below are based on a research report by *Tesev*, entitled *'Türkiye'de din, toplum ve siyaset'* (Religion, society and politics in Turkey) (Çarkoğlu and Toprak 2000). This investigation into the religious attitudes of the Turkish population indicates that the existence of a breeding ground for fundamentalism in Turkey is unlikely. Approximately one-third (35.2%) of Turks identify themselves first and foremost as Muslims. This figure differs widely between urban and rural people, and between people with higher and lower education levels. Those with little education in rural areas and smaller provincial towns, most frequently see themselves first and foremost as Muslims. Among people with higher education, only 10 per cent support this opinion. Fifty-three per cent of the population identify themselves first and foremost as citizens of Turkey, or as 'Turks'.

Examining how the Turks experience their faith, reveals that less than half of all men perform the compulsory five-times-a-day prayers, while about two-thirds participate in the Friday prayer, or at least say they do. This does not suggest great zeal. Furthermore, Turks seem to apply a flexible definition of the concept of 'Muslim'. Eighty-five per cent believe that someone who does not pray can still be classified as a Muslim. And 66 per cent do not view the consumption of alcohol (according to strict Islamic law, an offence punishable by flogging) as a disqualification from being a Muslim, while 85 per cent say that a woman who does not wear a headscarf can still be considered a Muslim. Thus, presentation and behaviour are not the most important criteria by which Turkish Muslims judge their fellow faithful.

Another criterion is whether people consider it problematic if Muslims and non-Muslims have to share the same personal or professional living environment. Roughly half of the Turkish people indicate that they prefer an environment in which people live according to the rules of Islam. When house-hunting, 54 per cent consider it important that their neighbours are religious, while 37 per cent do not. When there is a choice of two neighbourhood supermarkets, 49 per cent prefer the shop with a religious persuasion, 39 per cent have no preference for either. As far as friends are concerned, 61 per cent feel it is important that these are religious, while 31 per cent disagree. When it comes to professional life, 49 per cent agree that a religious person is more trustworthy and honest than a non-religious person, and 37 per cent disagree. (This could also be an important reason for preferring a 'religious' neighbourhood supermarket.)

The large majority of Turkish Muslims are fairly tolerant towards 'dissident thinkers': 89 per cent feel there are also 'good people' among the faithful of other religions. Sixty-three per cent of those interviewed do not want their son or daughter marrying a non-Muslim, so for over one-third, this is no insurmountable problem. A Muslim man, by the way, can happily marry a 'woman of the Book' under Islamic law, but it is not so simple for a Muslim women; her husband is required to convert to Islam.

It must be stressed that these questions related to non-Muslims did not distinguish between religions. It is thus quite possible that the so-called 'people of the Book' (Christians and Jews) are viewed more favourably by Turkish Muslims than, say, Hindus.

When it comes to the crucial issue of reintroducing the holy law into the family law, Turkish opinion is unanimous: don't! A mere 10 per cent of the population favour reintroducing Islamic marriages (and with it also the right to marry four women), while 14 per cent would like to see the return of Islamic divorce by repudiation.

The above data are of course no more than a fairly arbitrary summary of the figures, but the picture that emerges is that of a largely traditionally religious, but also relatively tolerant and not in the least fundamentalist, population. If we employ as the chief characteristic of fundamentalism the desire once again to base society on the şeriat (the Islamic law), then we can say that a maximum of between 10 and 15 per cent of the Turkish population are susceptible to fundamentalist thinking.

Other figures also seem to point in that direction. The large electoral success of the AK Party in the 2002 elections, can be attributed to the fact that the party emphatically distanced itself from the Islamic philosophy of Erbakan and his followers, and profiled itself as a broad, mainstream party, combining conservative standards and values with a belief in free markets, modernity and technology. Of those who voted for the AK Party, one segment had previously supported Erbakan's party, i.e. they were islamists. However, the Nationalist Action Party and the liberal-conservative Motherland Party also lost much support to the new AK Party. It thus represents a broad coalition. It is important that a party with such a profile even succeeded in soundly beating the 'real' Muslims of Erbakan's Felicity Party in his own home town, Konya, which is known as a devout town (Yavuz 2003: 258).

Support for truly militant groups, then, is small (see sect. 2.4). IBDA-C almost certainly does not have more than a few hundred dedicated followers, and possibly a few thousand sympathisers. The number of Hizbullah sympathisers has been estimated at 20,000, but this seems exaggerated. In Germany, home to more than three million Turks who can follow their political and religious preferences relatively freely and without the restrictions imposed by the Kemalist state apparatus, the radical 'State of the Caliphate' has never managed to attract more than about seven thousand followers. Obviously, this does not make such organisations less dangerous. As it turns out, only a handful of fanatics are needed for terrorist attacks. But it does indicate they do not find a breeding ground among the majority of the Turkish population. This means that the Turkish situation is fundamentally different from that in many Arab countries and in South and South-East Asia.

3.8 PLURALISM AS A COMPONENT OF DEMOCRATISATION

In the West, democracy is usually equated with pluralism, in all its aspects.
Here, we have mostly discussed Turkey's Islamic landscape, but we will
end this survey with a short account of the degree of pluralism in Turkey in
a wider sense.

The Turkish political system has democratic shortcomings due to electoral
thresholds, constitutional limitations, patronage systems and corruption.
The state's continuous pressure upon politics is indeed a problem, but
Turkey is still a country where voters can use the ballot box to bring to
power political groups other than those governing, and where the opposition can assume power peacefully. Voting is meaningful and there are clear
and viable political alternatives. Another characteristic democratic short-
coming in Turkey is censorship. The censor is still active on an almost daily
basis, when the authorities feel that newspapers or television stations have
overstepped their mark. Much like the Council for Higher Education
(YÖK), the Council for the Media (RTÜK) is one of the extensions with
which the state curbs civilian life. Publications by human rights organisations and organisations of Kurdish persuasion, in particular, are constantly
confronted with harassments. Nevertheless, Turkey has a large and richly
varied media, and its journalists and editors are continuously pushing the
bounds of possibility. Despite the censorship and self-censorship, it is
possible to find, buy and read strongly contrasting opinions on current
events from any street kiosk.

The economic sector also has its fair share of ambiguities. Over the last
25 years, Turkey's economic development has often been a process of all or
nothing. A very dynamic private sector, which includes tourism and
textiles, for example, functions alongside failing financial policies, such as
inefficient tax collecting and corruption. The annual growth of gross
national product has fluctuated between plus nine per cent and minus nine
per cent. Even so, all sections of Turkish society have become more prosperous during this period, and some spectacularly so.

This pluriformity of politics and the media is the product of a society that
has witnessed the rise of a large urban middle class whose prosperity
and education levels have grown enormously over the last 25 years, albeit
with ups and downs. The ideas of the state apparatus, with its heavy
emphasis on sovereignty and centralisation, are falling increasingly out
of step with a rapidly developing society. At the same time, however, that
very same state apparatus (including its 'Islamic branch', the Diyanet)
is also the heir to a massive administrative tradition stretching back some
700 years.

As far as the legitimacy of the state is concerned, it is important that Turkey never fell victim to colonial rule. Attempts in that direction were repelled by its population during the independence struggle of 1919-1922. In the recent past (since 1918), the country has not suffered any military defeats. As a result, the state never lost legitimacy in the eyes of its people. Many Turks are highly critical of their country, but they identify strongly with it, and are proud of its achievements.

3.9 THE TURKISH SITUATION: NEITHER 'THANKS TO ISLAM' NOR 'IN SPITE OF ISLAM'

If Turkey were to lose its status of a 'torn country' – to use Huntington's words – and were to become firmly anchored within Europe, that would be a truly hopeful message to the Islamic world; a sign that the 'clash of civilisations' is not a reality but a fantasy, and that the achievements of the West can also find a place in an Islamic country. However, this does not mean that the 'Turkish model' can simply be exported to other Islamic countries. For that, the Turkish experience is much too determined by specific historical factors. From a psychological perspective, too, it is unlikely that the countries in the Middle East will look to Turkey for a role model. Arab countries still see Turkey mainly as their former colonial ruler and as an accomplice of the imperialist West. The traditionally warm and, since the last decade, increasingly close relations of Turkey with their archenemy Israel, merely serve to reinforce this view. In fact, the Arab states have traditionally had much warmer relations with European countries such as Spain, Italy and Greece than with Turkey.

One final point: this survey is about Turkish Islam. It was undertaken to determine to what extent the fact that Turkey is an Islamic country will hinder its potential accession to the EU. In other words, whether the concept of the 'clash of civilisations' holds true. This concept defines 'Islam' as a civilisation confronting the West (and therefore Europe). This survey may therefore easily leave the impression that religion is the all-determining factor in Turkey's development. That is simply not true. Turkey is in many respects a modern country, where the originally Western concepts of democracy and human rights have taken root. True, this did not happen 'thanks to Islam', nor however 'in spite of Islam'. And when we look at other countries in the Islamic world, we must also resist the temptation to attribute their wrongs all too easily to religion. That is why it may be best to conclude this chapter with a quotation from Turkey's most prominent modern theologian, Mehmet Aydın, from an address made on 25 April 2001.

"In a society where individual rights are trampled on, society's moral dimension is also threatened, and even hindered. There are serious human rights abuses in the Islamic world, and its ruling Muslim classes are usually authoritarian. But religion as a social fact is only partially responsible for this situation. The roots of this problem of authoritarian governance must first be sought in the dominant political culture, in the unbearable economic situation, in the mazes and snares of international relations and, only then, in modern Islamic thoughts and actions.

To put it differently: religious pluralism can only be understood in conjunction with all other meaningful social factors. In a society where the constitutional state and social justice are acknowledged, and the need for democratic participation in government is met, a wide range of social roles is assigned to each citizen. Violence is systematically reduced and, eventually, a general political culture of constructive conflict management is applied. It is then that religion and religious life receive the opportunity to be truly religious and spiritual, and less, say, political and ideological. However, if these societal circumstances are lacking, then religious pluralism can never develop, not even if there are liberal tendencies within religious life" (Mehmet Aydın 2001: http://www.fleuri.ugent.be/cie/CIE/maydinnlı.htm).

167

4   CONCLUSION: TURKISH ISLAM AND EUROPEAN CIVILISATION

The reader who has read the above chapters of this survey, will not be surprised by the conclusions that are drawn below.

We first showed in chapter 2 that Turkish Islam has a long tradition of symbiosis with the state, and that this tradition has given 'official' Islam in Turkey a strongly pragmatic and flexible character. Another important characteristic of Islam in Turkey is its wide range of expressions. We have examined this extensively, and have indicated the importance of Turkey's large Alevi minority, with its adherence to secular and humanist values. We have seen how the large Islamic movements in Turkey that are not tied to the state, overwhelmingly try to combine their faith in modern science and technology with traditional standards and values. This is true for both the classic Dervish orders and for the neo-movements. The fact that these traditional standards and values are seen and experienced as 'Islamic', does not mean those movements are fundamentalist. There are truly radical fundamentalist groups in Turkey, but these are marginal. Admittedly, the attitude of the Islamic majority towards Turkey's minute Christian and Jewish minorities is problematic. However, the fact that religious preju-dices are diametrically opposed to the formal granting of equal treatment to all citizens, is not unique to Turkey. The same can be said of the attitude of Europeans to the Islamic minorities in Europe.

In chapter 3, we first tried to answer the question as to what extent Turkey is culturally a part of Europe. We began by concluding that the concept of identifiable civilisation blocs is not workable, and that the borders between civilisations are diffuse and porous. At the same time we stated that Turkey's modernisation has in effect also amounted to a long period of 'europeanisation', and that the legacies of Enlightenment and liberalism have also taken root in Turkey. From this point of departure, we answered the question whether Turkish Islam is compatible with political democracy and with the concept of human rights expressed in the European Conven-tion and the United Nation's Convention. Analysis of core texts of both official state-Islam and of Islam-inspired political mass movements show unambiguously that this is indeed the case. The documents of the current governing party explicitly refer to these conventions and use European practices as a yardstick. Where propagated values conflict with European values, this usually involves a glorification of the state and the military, and of authority in general, which bears no relation to Islam, even if Islam is used by the state to sanctify such values. In an Islamic context, it is hard to conceive of a complete separation of state and religion. However, it will

169

certainly prove necessary to readjust the message of state-Islam into a more 'civil' direction.

It should come as no surprise that both state-linked and non-state linked mainstream Islam in Turkey have a message that is moderate, flexible, and reasonably tolerant. Sociological research into the religious attitudes of the population confirms this picture. If we combine this research with political data such as election results and research into illegal organisations, we can safely conclude that a maximum of 15 per cent of the Turkish population feel attracted to (elements of) fundamentalist thought. Support for such (illegal) movements that also justify the use of violence, is probably very small.

In a religious and more general cultural sense, Turkey exhibits a number of characteristics that closely correspond to those present in some parts of Europe. This is not only understandable from its long history of contact with Europe and the deliberate ambition of the Turkish elite to become European, but also from the characteristics of modern-day Turkish society, with its large and mature urban middle class, political pluralism and strong growth of prosperity. The fact that Turkey's dominant religion is Islam, not Christianity, does not change this, nor does the fact that it tends to have more in common with countries such as Poland or Greece than with, say, the Netherlands or Denmark. To exclude Turkey on the basis of cultural and religious criteria, as suggested by European politicians and writers who allow themselves to be inspired by Huntington's ideas, is therefore wrong. Turkey's alleged un-European character is a construction, based on a very shaky definition of a European or 'Western' civilisation, and on a poor understanding of Turkish reality.

This is not to say that there are no objections against Turkey's EU accession. Arguments relating to poverty, migration and the decision-making capacity of European institutions must be taken seriously. This survey does not cover these aspects. It is merely concerned with the argument (unfounded, in our view) that Turkey could not, or should not, become a member *because* the large majority of its population is Muslim.

LITERATURE

Abu Manneh, B. (1979) 'Sultan Abdülhamid II and Shaikh Abdulhuda Al-Sayyadi' in *Middle Eastern Studies*, 15.

AK Parti (2003) Her şey AK Türkiye için. Seçim beyannamesi, Ankara: AK Parti.

Anderson, B. (1991) *Imagined communities*, London: Verso.

Aydın, M. (2001) http://www.fleuri.ugent.be/cie/CIE/maydinnlı.htm

Bali, R. (1999) Cumhuriyet yıllarında Türkiye Yahudileri. Bir türkleştirme serüveni (1923-1945), Istanbul: Iletişim.

Birge, J.K. (1937) *The Bektaşi order of derwishes*, London: Hartfort.

Braude, B. and B. Lewis (eds.) (1982) *Christians and Jews in the Ottoman Empire. The functioning of a plural society*, New York: Holmes & Meier.

Bruinessen, M. van (1996) 'Kurds, Turks and the Alevi revival in Turkey' in *Middle East Report*, 26, 3.

Buitelaar, M. and J. ter Haar (eds.) (1999) *Mystiek. Het andere gezicht van de islam*, Bussum: Coutinho.

Çamuroğlu, R. (1997) 'Some notes on the contemporary process of restructuring Alevilik in Turkey' in Kehl-Bodrogi, Kellner-Heinkele, Otter-Beaujean (eds.), *Syncretistic religious communities in the Near East*, Leiden: Brill, 25-34.

Cantwell Smith, W. (1957) *Islam in modern history*, Princeton: Princeton University Press.

Çarkoğlu, A. and B. Toprak (2000) *Türkiye'de din, toplum ve siyaset, Istanbul: tesev Yayınları*.

Cumhuriyet (2001) 'Erkek artık evin reisi değil', 22 June.

Deringil, S. (1998) *The well-protected domains. Ideology and the legitimation of power in the Ottoman Empire 1876-1909*, London: I.B. Taurus.

Douwes, D. (1997) 'Richtingen en stromingen' in Henk Driessen (ed.), *In het huis van de islam*, Nijmegen: Sun, 162-181.

Driessen, H. (ed.) (1997) *In het huis van de Islam*, Nijmegen: Sun.

Dumont, P. (1984) 'The origins of Kemalist ideology' in Jacob M. Landau (ed.), *Atatürk and the modernization of Turkey*, Boulder: Westview, 25-44.

Ekster, J. den (1990) *Diyanet. Een reis door de keuken van de officiële Turkse Islam*, Beverwijk: Centrum Buitenlanders Peregrinus.

Erbakan, N. (1975) *Millî Görüş*, Istanbul: Dergâh Yayınları.

Erdoğan, N. (2000) 'Kemalist non-governmental organizations. Troubled elites in defence of a sacred heritage' in Stefanos Yerasimos et al. (eds.), *Civil society in the grip of nationalism*, Istanbul: Orient-Institut, 283-334.

Evren, K. (1986) *Türkiye Cumhuriyeti Devlet Başkanı Orgeneral Kenan Evren'in söylev ve demeçleri: 1985-1986*, Ankara: Başbakanlık.

Geoffroy, E. 'Tarika' in *Encyclopaedia of Islam, New Edition*, vol. X, Leiden: Brill, 243-6.

Georgeon, F. (ed.) (2000) *Les mots de politique de l'Empire Ottoman à la Turquie kemaliste*, Paris: ehess/esa 8032, cnrs.

171

Gezik, E. (2000) *Alevi Kürtler*, Ankara: Kalan.

Göle, N. (1996) *The forbidden modern. Civilization and veiling*, Michigan: The University of Michigan Press.

Groot, A.H. de (1986) *Nederland en Turkije. Zeshonderd jaar politieke, economische en culturele contacten*, Leiden: Nederlands Instituut voor het Nabije Oosten.

Hanioğlu, M.Ş. (1995) *The Young Turks in opposition, opposition*, Oxford: Oxford University Press.

Hanioğlu, M.Ş. (1997) 'Garbcılar. Their attitudes toward religion and their impact on the official ideology of the Turkish Republic', *Studia Islamica*, 86, 2: 133-158.

Hobsbawm, E. (1990) *Nations and nationalism since 1780. Programme, myth, reality*, Cambridge: Cambridge University Press.

Hoebink, M. (1997) 'Het denken over vernieuwing en secularisatie' in Henk Driessen (ed.), *In het huis van de Islam*, Nijmegen: Sun, 199-217.

Huntington, S. (2002), *The Clash of Civilizations and the Remaking of the World Order*, London: The Free Press.

Imber, C. (1997) *Ebu's-su'ud: The Islamic legal tradition*, Edinburgh: Edinburgh University Press.

Imber, C. (2002) *The Ottoman Empire, 1300-1650. The structure of power*, New York: Palgrave Macmillan.

Jansen, J.J.G. (1998) *Nieuwe inleiding tot de Islam*, Bussum: Coutinho.

Kafadar, C. (1995) *Between two worlds. The construction of the Ottoman state*, Berkeley: University of California Press.

Karpat, K.H. (ed.) (2000) *Ottoman past and today's Turkey*, Leiden: Brill.

Karpat, K.H. (2001) 'Nursî' in *Encyclopaedia of Islam. New Edition*, vol. VIII, Leiden: Brill: 143-4.

Kehl-Bodrogi, K., B. Kellner-Heinkele and A. Otter-Beaujean (eds.) (1997) *Syncretistic religious communities in the Near East*, Leiden: Brill.

Lewis, B. (1996) *Het Midden-Oosten. 2000 jaar culturele en politieke geschiedenis*, Amsterdam: Forum.

Mardin, Ş. (1998) *Religion and social change in modern Turkey. The case of Bediüzzaman Said Nursi*, New York: State University of New York.

Ocak, A. (1997) 'Un aperçu général sur l'hétérodoxie musulmane en Turquie' in Kehl-Bodrogi, Kellner-Heinkele, Otter-Beaujean (eds.), *Syncretistic religious communities in the Near East*, Leiden: Brill: 195-204.

Olsson, T., E. and C.R. Özdalga (eds.) (1999) *Alevi kimliği*, Istanbul: Tarih Vakfı Yurt Yayınları.

Özdemir, A. and K. Frank (2000) *Visible Islam in modern Turkey*, London: Macmillan.

Parla, R. (1985) *Türkiye Cumhuriyeti'nin uluslararası temelleri*, Nicosia: private.

Poulton, H. (1997) *Top hat, grey wolf and crescent*, London: Hurst & Company.

Şener, C. (1990) *Alevilik olayı: toplumsal bir başkaldırının kısa tarihçesi*, Istanbul: Alev Yayınevi.

Shankland, D. (1999) *Islam and society in Turkey*, Cambridgeshire: The Eothen Press.

Shindeldecker, J. (2000) *Turkish Alevis today*, www.isik.ch

Soymen, M. (2000) *Cep ilmihali, Ankara:* Diyanet İşleri Başkanlığı Yayınları.

Sunier, Th. (1998) *Turkije. Mensen, politiek, economie, cultuur*, Amsterdam: Koninklijk Instituut voor de Tropen.

Toprak, B. (1981) *Islam and political development in Turkey*, Leiden: Brill.

Yavuz, M.H. (2003) *Islamic political identity in Turkey*, New York: Oxford University Press.

Yerasimos, S. et al. (eds.) (2000) *Civil society in the grip of nationalism*, Istanbul: Orient-Institut.

Zarcone, Th. (2001) 'Tasawwuf. Among the Turks', *Encyclopaedia of Islam*. New Edition, vol. X, Leiden: Brill: 332-4.

Zürcher, E.J. (1993) *Turkey: A modern history*, London: I.B. Taurus.

Zürcher, E.J. (1995) *Een geschiedenis van het moderne Turkije*, Nijmegen: Sun.

Zürcher, E.J. (1997), 'Islam en politiek: Turkije' in Henk Driessen (ed.), *In het huis van de Islam*, Nijmegen: Sun.

Zürcher, E.J. (2000) 'Young Turks, Ottoman Muslims and Turkish nationalists. Identity politics 1908-1938' in K. H. Karpat (ed.), *Ottoman past and today's Turkey*, Leiden: Brill: 150-179.

Zürcher, E.J. (2000) 'The core terminology of Kemalism. Mefkûre, millî, muasır, medenî' in: F. Georgeon (ed.) Les mots de politique de l'Empire Ottoman à la Turquie kemaliste, Paris: ehess/esa 8032 cnrs: 55-64.

Zürcher, E.J., 'Ottoman sources of Kemalist thought', http://www.let.leidenuniv.nl/tcimo/tulp (working papers archive).

173

WEBSITES

http://www.ict.org.il Great East Islamic Raiders Front (IBDA-C) (4-12-2003)
http://www.im.nrw.de Innenministerium nrw – 'Kalifatstat', 'Kaplan' (4-12-2003)
http://www.terrorism.com The Terrorism Research Center – 'Turkish Hizballah'
    (3-12-2003)
http://www.let.leidenuniv.nl/tcimo/tulp 'Turkology Update Leiden Project'